CLASSIC WWI AIRCRAFT PROFILES

CLASSIC WWI
AIRCRAFT PROFILES

Volume Two

CERBERUS

Published in 2002

PUBLISHED IN THE UNITED KINGDOM BY:

Cerberus Publishing Limited
Penn House, Leigh Woods
Bristol BS8 3PF
Telephone: ++44 117 974 7175
Facsimile: ++44 117 973 0890
e-mail: cerberusbooks@aol.com

British Library Cataloguing in Publication Data.
A catalogue record for this book is available from the British Library.

ISBN 1 84145 102 9

PRINTED AND BOUND IN ITALY

Contents

Introduction

World War One could well be considered the first 'modern' war as, apart from the de-humanising aspects of trench warfare, it introduced the tank and the aircraft, both of which came to be the dominating factors in the conduct of subsequent wars and battles.

The aircraft available, at the outbreak of World War One, were little more than 'box' kites and had been developed for sport rather than a weapon of war. When, in 1914, the various military authorities of the protagonists considered the possibilities of using aircraft it was primarily in the rôle of transportation for 'observers' to reconnôitre troop movements. Officers, who were 'gentlemen', conducted the observation while the 'driver', invariably a non-commissioned officer and trained as a mechanic, flew the aircraft on the instructions of his passenger.

At the onset of war in August 1914, it was Germany and France that had the largest number of aircraft and, in Germany's case, airships. The combined total from both the Imperial German Air Service and the Imperial Naval Air Service amounted to under 300 machines and nearly half of this total were *Taube* (Dove) aircraft originally designed by an Austrian engineer Igo Etrich in 1910. French enthusiasts had taken a keen interest in developing 'flying machines' from the earliest days of manned flight and produced many innovative features that were incorporated into the designs of aircraft throughout the world. But, even they could only muster around 160 aircraft and 15 airships at the outbreak of war.

Such was the state of the Allies' (Belgium and Russia) aircraft industry in 1914 that they had to rely, heavily, on French production, therefore much of the early aerial activity was conducted with French machines. Belgium, when they were invaded on August 4, 1914, had less than 20 aircraft and suitable only for reconnaissance purposes. The Imperial Russian Air Service had around 240 aircraft, many of which were of French design and production and to this the imperial Russian Navy could add a small quantity of floatplanes and flying boats.

The British government was also caught unawares and, in the early months of the war, had also to rely heavily on French machines. The British Imperial General Staff had no concept of modern warfare and decided that should the aeroplane have a rôle it would be for obsrvation and reconnaissance. A few years earlier, in 1913, Major Brooke-Popham of the Air Battalion, Royal Engineers, did see the possibilities of 'aerial combat' and bolted a gun, in a fixed position, to his Blériot monoplane. This 'ungentlemanly' act was soon censured by his superior officers and he was ordered to remove it. About the same time the designer and manufacturer of machine-guns, Colonel Isaac Newton Lewis, demonstrated the possibilities of using the aeroplane as an offensive weapon by fitting one of his machine-guns on a Wright biplane belonging to the U.S. Army Signal Corps. Such was the reception that he left the country in disgust and subsequently established a factory in Liège, Belgium, to manufacture his guns.

The crews of the first Royal Flying Corps aircraft to be sent to France were, therefore, required to report on the enemy's troop and artillery movements but, should they encounter any Zeppelins, they were authorised to ram them! This hazardous pastime was met with very little enthusiasm by the crews, especially as parachutes and life jackets did not form part of their kit.

Early 'scout' aircraft of the German, French and British air services had the manoeuvrability to engage in combat but their crews were usually equipped with hand-guns. These needed to be fired at point-blank range and, even then, with a huge amount of luck. It was of course the machine-gun that provided the impetus and by early 1915 the Lewis and Hotchkiss machine-guns were being fitted to the Allied aircraft, later to be joined by Vickers. German machines had the LMG Parabellum, also known as the Spandau, fitted. Although these gave some form of armament there was a limitation on their use by the pilot as they were usually fitted on the top wing - to avoid shattering the propeller - or at an upward angle. Either way it needed great skill by the pilot as he would invariably have to stand in the cockpit, holding his control column between his knees, before he could fire his gun. More accuracy was achieved by the observer as his machine-gun could be turned and pivoted thus allowing him a wider range within which to fire.

It was not until the interrupter gear, allowing the machine-gun to fire through the propeller, that 'fighter' aircraft came of age. This innovation soon allowed pilots on both sides to amass 'scores' of the aircraft they shot down, and names such as Boelcke, Immelmann, Richthofen, Guynemer, Nungesser, Ball, Mannock, Bishop and Rickenbacker were soon receiving a hero's adulation.

Classic WWI Aircraft Profiles gives a short history, in text and illustrations, of many of the aircraft flown by these heroes.

CHAPTER ONE

The Bristol Fighter

In July 1916 the British Army stood ready and awaiting orders to advance along the River Somme, cross and drive the German forces back. The German Army stood awaiting the expected onslaught as both sides prepared for a set battle. Large numbers of men, guns and ammunition were assembled, reinforcements in place to give support to the front line troops when required, and in the air there was much movement as both sides sent over the reconnaissance aircraft which would be met by nimble fighters.

The Royal Flying Corps (R.F.C.), at this time, stood ready with a total of approximately 450 aircraft of all types, of which just 80 were single-seat fighters. The remainder mainly consisted of reconnaissance two-seaters, fighters and bombers, but it proved to be an inadequate force to hold off German Air Force machines.

Several months after the start of the conflict the fledgling R.F.C. had recognised that their 'flying-machines' were fast becoming outdated and a liability when confronting the innovative and dedicated production of German aircraft. In the light of this the R.F.C. had demanded a new and effective replacement for the lumbering B.E.2s. They asked for up-dated designs which, in addition to the ability to carry out normal reconnaissance and artillery spotting, plus fighters to protect them, the new replacements had to be capable of defending itself against the marauding German fighters.

As a replacement for the B.E.2 the Royal Aircraft Factory had designed the R.E.8. The prototype of which flew for the first time in June 1916 but was not a great advance on the 'redundant' B.Es. Following a few modifications and approval of the design the first production aircraft was completed by September of that year, too late to have an effect on the Battle of the Somme, and large numbers of the subsequent production run proved quite unsatisfactory in operation.

During the same period, approximately March 1916 and just four months before the forthcoming battle, Captain Barnwell, Chief Designer of the British and Colonial Aircraft Company based in Bristol, had started work on the design of a two-seat tractor biplane which was intended to be a replacement for the B.E. two-seaters as a reconnaissance aircraft. Additionally, the new type was to be capable of carrying out fighting patrols.

The designation Bristol R.2A was applied to this design, which was to have the 120-hp Beardmore engine. Dual controls were to be fitted, and a camera and wireless were included in the machine's equipment. The wings were of 40 ft 8 in. span, and the fuselage was to have been mounted mid-way between them in order to bring the pilot's eye level with the upper wing. The designed armament consisted of two Lewis machine-guns: one was fixed on the starboard upper longeron and was synchronised to fire forward through the airscrew, while the observer had a Scarff ring-mounting for his gun.

The prototype Bristol F.2A (A3303) which evolved into the prototype F2B.

It was recognised that the R.2A, as good as it was, would be under-powered with the 120-hp Beardmore engine and Captain Barnwell, therefore, considered the substitution of a Hispano-Suiza engine. However, a new Rolls-Royce 'vee'-twelve engine, of 190-hp, later to achieve fame as the Falcon, became available at this time and was soon installed in the prototype aircraft.

In configuration, size and output the Falcon engine was ideal for Barnwell's purpose, but with characteristic thoroughness he did not merely modify the R.2A to accommodate the new engine. He produced what was virtually a new design that took full advantage of the Rolls-Royce engine. This new design was designated Bristol F.2A.

The fuselage remained in the mid-gap position: thus the pilot had the widest possible field of vision. A single fixed Vickers machine-gun was mounted under the cowling, on the aircraft's centre-line, and was synchronised to fire through the propeller arc. The fuselage was redesigned to terminate aft in a horizontal knife-edge, and the tail-unit also underwent revision. Thus the observer was given a wide field of fire for his Lewis gun, as he could fire forwards over the upper wing with very little elevation of his gun, and the downward sweep of the top of the fuselage left very little blind area to the rear. The aeroplane was essentially a fighter, and 'Bristol Fighter' became the synonymous name by which it gained renown.

The initial order was for two prototypes (A3303 and A3304), one with the Rolls-Royce Falcon Mk.1, the other with the 150-hp Hispano-Suiza engine. A contract was also placed for fifty production machines with the serials A3305 to A3354. Construction began in July 1916, just as the Battle of the Somme was launched, and the first prototype, A3303, was completed by September 9, 1916.

In its original form A3303 had two long vertical radiators, one on either side of the fuselage and there were short exhaust manifolds with forward outlets. The engine drove a substantial four-bladed left-hand airscrew. However, it was soon found that the radiators obscured part of the pilot's

F.2A, A3304, the second prototype at Filton, December 1916. Note the filled in lower gap between the wings. This aircraft was eventually modified to become the second prototype with the new, circular radiator.

field of vision, particularly for landing. They were therefore replaced by a flat radiator of more or less circular shape installed in the nose of the fuselage, which was modified to conform to the contour of the new radiator. The exhaust manifolds were revised to provide a rear outlet for the gases, and the machine was later flown with a two-bladed left-hand airscrew. The end plates were removed from the lower wing roots and a shallow coaming fitted around the cockpits.

Prototype A3303 went to the Central Flying School at Upavon, in the second week of October 1916 and it flew with a four-blade propeller that had

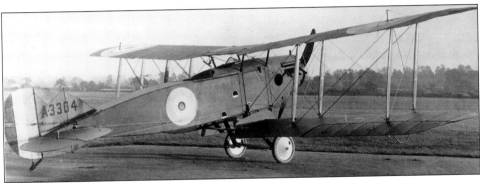

The second prototype F.2A (A3304)

a diameter of 9 ft 2 in. This was followed by trials at the experimental armament establishment at Orfordness with a Scarff ring-mounting on the rear cockpit and an Aldis sight for the forward Vickers machine-gun.

A3304, the second prototype that had the 150-hp Hispano-Suiza engine, was ready for flight testing by October 25, 1916, and was fitted with a circular nose-type radiator from the beginning. A minor point of difference between the two prototypes was that the A3304 had its tailskid built into the base of the rudder, whereas the first machine had a pylon-type unit generally similar to that of the B.E. biplanes.

Both prototypes had mainplanes similar in plan to those of the B.E.2C, and neither had the lower centre-section covered in: the lower wings were attached to an open cross-braced steel tube structure which was known as the wing anchorage frame. Each prototype originally had a vertical end-plate at the inboard end of each lower mainplane, but these surfaces were later removed. In both prototypes the pilot's seat was armoured.

The Bristol F.2A passed its official trials with complete success, and returned performance figures which were better than the estimates. Fifty

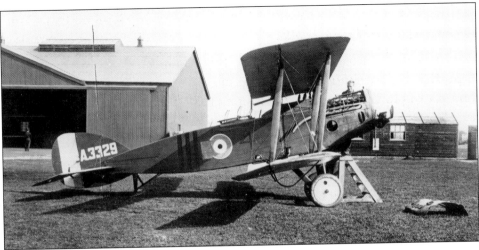

Bristol F.2A (A3329) pictured at Beaulieu.

production machines were ordered and were powered by the Rolls-Royce Falcon engine since no Hispano-Suizas were available; at that time all available engines of the latter type were wanted for S.E.5s.

The production F.2As, numbered A3305 to A3354, were almost identical to the A3303, the second prototype, but the plan-form of the wing-tips was modified to a simpler, blunt outline, which remained standard on all succeeding variants. The lower centre-section remained an open structure, and a two-bladed right-hand airscrew was used. No armour was fitted to the pilot's seat in production F.2As.

Production aircraft deliveries started in December 1916 and the first R.F.C. squadron to receive them was No. 48. To provide pilots and observers with familiarisation on the new Bristol Fighter, members of No. 48 Squadron had received training at central Flying School, Rendcombe. They, therefore, became the first unit to take the machine to France, arriving at Bellevue on

A development of the F.2 was the MR.1. The first machine, A5177, is of all metal construction.

March 8 and settled down to await the imminent Battle of Arras. The Squadron's first offensive patrol was made on April 5, 1917, but, unfortunately, this proved to be a disastrous debut for the Bristol.

The patrol consisted of six F.2As and was led by Captain W. Leefe-Robinson, V.C. Over Douai, they were attacked by five Albatros D.IIIs led by Manfred von Richthofen, the 'Red Baron'. He shot down two of the Bristols for his thirty-fifth and thirty-sixth victories and two others, one of them flown by Leefe-Robinson himself, were accounted for by Richthofen's pilots. In his combat report Richthofen wrote of A3340, flown by Lieutenant A. M. Leckler (observer, Lieutenant H. D. K. George) and was the first of the two

F.2As he shot down, that although this new aeroplane was fast and capable of defending, his D.III Albatros was undoubtedly superior.

By April 16 eight more Bristol F.2As had been lost (five of them through overstaying their patrol and running out of fuel), and opinion at RFC Headquarters must have been somewhat similar to Richthofen's judgement.

But the fault lay not in the Bristol. In its earliest days, its crews, Leefe-Robinson's patrol included, made the serious tactical error of flying the machine in the accepted manner of the time for two-seaters; namely, as a platform for the observer's gun. They failed to recognise the Bristol's supreme combat virtues of manoeuvrability and structural strength.

Fortunately, one or two pilots began, more-or-less experimentally, to fight with the Bristol in the single-seat fashion, using the front gun as the primary weapon and leaving the observer to protect the tail. These tactics were immediately successful, and were forthwith adopted by No. 48 Squadron and by No. 11, the second unit to receive Bristol Fighters. The leading exponent of the Bristol Fighter was Lieutenant A. E. McKeever of No. 11 Squadron,

Bristol F.2A of No.. 48 Squadron.

who opened his scoring on June 19, 1917, by shooting down an Albatros Scout. McKeever ultimately shot down thirty enemy aircraft, and won nearly all of his victories on the Bristol Fighter.

The first weeks of operational flying indicated certain desirable modifications, chief among which was the need to improve the pilot's forward view. This was achieved by sloping the upper longerons downwards from the front of the observer's cockpit to the level of the engine bearers. this modification permitted the installation of a larger fuel tank and cowling with a narrow top. The modified fuselage was tested on A.3304, the second F.2A prototype, which retained its Hispano-Suiza engine. At the same time, the lower centre-section was built out to full aerofoil section and covered.

All production machines from A.7101 onwards had the revised fuselage and covered lower centre-section, and were given new designation, the Bristol F.2B. The first 150 F.2Bs (A.7101-A.7250) had the 190-hp Rolls-Royce Falcon I engine, with the exception of A.7177, in which the first installation of the 275-hp Rolls-Royce Falcon III engine was made. The second Bristol F.2B to have the Falcon III was A.7183, which was later fitted with the more powerful

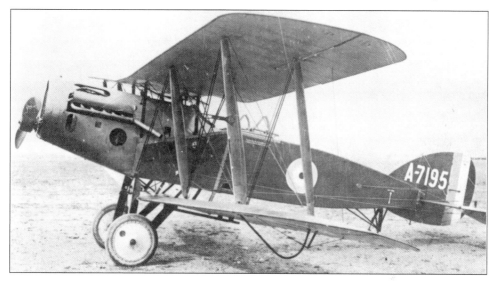

F.2B, A7195, of the first production batch was delivered to No.. 48 Squadron.

engine. The first few F.2Bs had no radiator shutters but these were soon standardised. A further modification was the introduction of a new horizontal tail of reduced chord and increased span.

Production continued with fifty machines (A.7251-A.7300) powered by the 220-hp Rolls-Royce Falcon II, and all subsequent Bristols, from B.1101 onwards were intended to have the Falcon III. In 1917, however, Rolls-Royce engines were not being produced in sufficient quantities to meet the growing demands of the time. The realisation of the excellence of the Bristol Fighter led to a substantial expansion of production of the type, and by the Autumn of 1917 it was obvious that Falcon production would not be able to keep pace with the output of Bristol Fighters.

Alternative power units had to be considered, and the first choice was the 200-hp Hispano-Suiza. It was realised that this lower-powered engine would reduce the aircraft's performance, so it was decided to use the Hispano Bristols as replacements for the R.E.8 and Armstrong Whitworth F.K.8. in the Corps Reconnaissance squadrons. The Falcon-powered machines were to be reserved for the fighter-reconnaissance squadrons, whose duties demanded the best possible performance.

However, the 200-hp Hispano-Suiza was giving a great deal of trouble in 1917, as the pilots of the early S.E.5a's knew only too well. Those engines made in France by the Brasier concern proved to be woefully defective, particularly in the hardening of the gears and airscrew shaft. Facilities for their overhaul in Britain became so over-taxed and the engine supply position so critical that many Brasier-built Hispano-Suizas were passed into service with the faulty gears.

This F.2B, D7966, of No.. 139 Squadron, was captured by the Austrians. Flown by Lt C E G Gill and Lt T Newey.

To have fitted appreciable numbers of Bristol Fighters with these Hispano-Suiza engines would have been to invite catastrophe, and the aircraft was modified to have 200-hp Sunbeam Arab engine. The Arab was a liquid-cooled 'vee'-eight of generally similar configuration to the Hispano-Suiza.

The original Arab installation bore a strong external resemblance to that of the Wolseley Viper version of the S.E.5a, and was in fact an attempt to use S.E.5a radiators which were readily available. The nose was flat and square with an arched top, and there was one radiator block for each group of cylinders. The top line of the engine cowling sloped down quite sharply to the top of the radiator, and it was felt that this resulted in the blast-tube for the Vickers gun being too short. The nose lines were revised to give a horizontal top line to the cowling, and the end elevation of the nose resembled a rectangle surmounted by a shallow inverted 'V'; the appearance was

Bristol F.2B, C906, with Sunbeam Arab engine, Filton, April 1918. Twin radiator blocks as for the Wolseley Viper engine installation.

exceedingly ugly. An improvement was made by redesigning the nose so that it became straight-sided with rounded top and bottom; but at the last minute this was further modified to enable the cowling to accommodate either the Sunbeam Arab or the 300-hp Hispano-Suiza. Availability of the latter engine was promised in July 1918.

Mere modifications of the cowling were by no means the only worries connected with the Sunbeam Arab. The engine had given trouble from its earliest days. In the spring of 1917 several modifications had to be made to overcome weaknesses of the crank chamber and cylinders, and even then the Arab was so unsatisfactory that it was nearly shelved. After one engine had

HM Queen Mary on a visit to St Omer Depot, July 1917.

satisfactorily completed a test run of 100 hours on the bench, development proceeded, but many more modifications had to be made and specifications for materials had to be changed. As a result, the design of the engine was not settled until late in 1917, by the end of the year only eighty-one Arabs had been delivered against the production programme total of 1,800. The engine suffered severely from vibration at normal operating speeds, and even the introduction of specially strengthened engine mountings in the Bristol Fighter airframe failed to achieve a fully satisfactory combination.

The adoption of the Sunbeam Arab coincided with the extension of production of the Bristol Fighter to sub-contractors, and that engine was selected as the power unit of the machines ordered under the first two outside contracts, which were placed with the Gloucester Aircraft Co., Ltd, on October 30, 1917, and with Marshall & Sons of Gainsborough on November 22, 1917. On the latter date, a contract was also given to the Cunard Steamship Co., for the construction of 500 Bristol Fighters with the 200-hp Hispano-Suiza engine. The factory, which Cunard erected for the purpose at Aintree, was taken over in February 1918, by the Ministry of Munitions, and was thereafter known as National Aircraft Factory No. 3. Production did not begin at Aintree until March 1918, and only 126 Bristol

F.2B (B1148) of No. .1 Squadron AFC.

Fighter airframes were completed there.

Further contracts for Arab-powered machines were let on February 22, 1918, with the Standard Motor Co., Armstrong Whitworth & Co., and Angus Sanderson & Co. These were followed on March 20 by a second contract for 150 machines from the Gloucester Aircraft Co., and on May 21 by a contract for 100 to be built by Harris & Sheldon.

As previously stated, it was intended to fit the 300-hp Hispano-Suiza engine to the Bristol Fighter, and with the promise of such engines in July, 1918, a batch of 350 Fighters were put in hand. Work on these machines had begun when it was found that all 300-hp Hispano-Suiza engines were wanted for the Martinsyde F.4 production programme.

E2459 was flown by Lt F Jeffries and by C M B Martin of No. 88 Squadron.

Yet another change was made. This time the choice fell, almost with a suggestion of desperation, on the 230-hp Siddeley Puma six-cylinder in-line engine. The Bristol F.2B numbered B.1206 was tested with a Puma in February 1918. At the time the installation bore a general resemblance to that

F.2, B1134, '19, of No.. 35 Squadron.

of the Falcon, for the frontal radiator was retained. A large exhaust manifold was fitted on the port side, and the Vickers gun had to be mounted to starboard of the cylinders.

The exhaust manifold and the gun obstructed the pilot's forward view. The official test report suggested, therefore, that the engine installation should be modified to be similar to that of the D.H.9, and that an under-slung radiator or twin side radiator should replace the frontal surface.

Most of the recommendations were implemented, and by September 1918, the necessary modifications had been made to enable production Bristols to

F.2B of No. .11 Squadron showing the Scarff ring.

accommodate the Puma. In addition to the modifications to the cowling itself, the fuel tanks had to be completely redesigned and a massive exhaust manifold was fitted.

The British & Colonial Aeroplane Company fitted Pumas to the machines numbered E.3253-E.3258 and H.1690-H.1707 at Filton near Bristol, but none of these went further than the Aircraft Acceptance Park. Puma-powered Bristols were also built by the Gloucester concern and by the Austin Motor Company.

In September, 1918, trials were carried out with the Bristol Fighter C.4654 powered by one of the high-compression Siddeley Pumas which developed 290-hp. The installation of this more powerful engine was indistinguishable from that of the standard Puma and the improvement in performance was of little significance.

In all these circumstances it is not surprising that the first deliveries of Bristol Fighters to Corps Reconnaissance units did not take place until September 1918, whereas it had been planned to replace the R.E.8s from the previous April onwards. Five of the Corps squadrons in France had had one

F.2B of No. .8 Squadron based at Malincourt, November 1918.

or two Bristols on their strength as early as March 21, 1918. Squadrons Nos 10 and 35 (Armstrong Whitworth F.K.8) and No. 16 (R.E.8) each had two, and Nos 12 and 15 (R.E.8) each had one. But no Corps squadron was ever re-equipped with Bristol Fighters, the only units which used the Arab-powered version in France were the Long Range Artillery Flights L, M, N, O and P. Of these L Flight was the first to join the British Expeditionary Forces (B.E.F.) and it arrived in France in July 1918. Of the 721 Arab-Bristols on the charge of the R.A.F. on October 31, 1918, only seventy-nine were with the Expeditionary Force in France.

A few experimental Bristol Fighters had the 200-hp RAF 4d engine. This was an air-cooled 'vee'-twelve which did not lend itself to elegant cowling, and the installation was by no means beautiful.

At least one Bristol Fighter, B.1200, was tested in October 1918, with the 200-hp Wolseley Viper engine. Performance was poor, however, and no attempt was made to standardise the viper.

It was in its standard fighter-reconnaissance form with the Rolls-Royce

F.2B B1146 of No. .1 Squadron in the Western Desert.

Falcon engine that the Bristol Fighter won its undying fame. Once its great strength and manoeuvrability were realised and exploited by its pilots, it became one of the most effective weapons in the armoury of the R.F.C., and so far redressed the early losses Of April 1917, that by the time of the Armistice No. 48 Squadron had destroyed 148 enemy aircraft. The crews of No. 11 Squadron found that they could not bring the enemy to battle unless the Bristols flew in pairs or singly, enemy pilots would not attack if more than three of No. 11's machines were flying together.

In the summer of 1917, the Bristol Fighters of No. 48 Squadron escorted the D.H.4s of No. 5 (Naval) Squadron on many bombing raids, and twice during

F.2B of No.. 11 Squadron as flown by A P MacLean and his observer G Canthon.

Bristol F.2B, A7231, which was captured by the Germans., who applied their national markings.

Another captured F.2B with the words 'Do Not Shoot, Good People'

that year one of No. 48's Bristols carried as its observer King Albert of Belgium, who wished to see the battlefield for himself.

The Bristol Fighter gave excellent service throughout the Battle of Ypres, and in September 1917, No. 48 Squadron began to fly at night to attempt to intercept the German bombers which attacked Dunkirk. This squadron had earlier scored a success against Gothas which were returning from a daylight raid on Harwich, on July 22, 1917, Captain B.E.Baker and his observer, Lieutenant G.R.Spencer, dived to the attack from 16,000 ft to 3,000 ft and

Major Barker flying F.2B of No.. 139 Squadron.

shot down one of the Gothas into the sea.

The great German offensive of 1918 brought fresh tasks to the Bristol Fighter squadrons. Ground targets were plentiful, and No. 48 Squadron was in the thick of the ground attack work, whilst Nos. 11, 22 and 62 plied their craft at any altitude where there was fighting to be done.

Eloquent testimony to the confidence that Bristol crews had in their machines was provided on May 7, 1918, when two of No. 22 Squadron's pilots attacked seven Fokkers over Arras. Four of the German fighters had fallen to the Bristol's guns when fifteen more enemy fighters appeared. Only the exhaustion of their ammunition obliged the Bristol Fighters to break off the engagement, and by that time they had shot down four more Fokkers.

In Italy, No. 139 Squadron's Bristols distinguished themselves against odds, on August 8, 1918, when four machines of that unit beat off an onslaught by twenty enemy fighters. No. 139 Squadron began its career as a Flight of Bristol Fighters which was sent to Italy in Spring 1918 in compensation for the transfer to the Western Front of No. 42 (R.E.8) Squadron, but it was soon transferred to No. 34 Squadron and named 'Z' Flight. A second Bristol Flight arrived in June, and the two were named No. 139 Squadron on July 3, 1918.

Farther east, in Palestine, Bristol Fighters gave the R.F.C. their first real opportunity of carrying the war to the enemy in the autumn of 1917, when a few were sent there. Five Bristols were serviceable on October 7, and on that day the first offensive patrol was made. On the next day, the first German fighter to be captured on the Sinai-Palestine Front was brought down in the British lines. By October 27, 1917, No. 111 Squadron had six Bristol Fighters on its strength, these machines were handed over to No. 67 (Australian) Squadron, R.F.C. in January 1918, when that unit was re-equipped. No. 67 Squadron became No. 1 Squadron, Australian Flying Corps, on February 6, 1918. The only other Bristol Fighter which saw operational service in the Middle East was the solitary example which was used by 'X' Flight at El Gueira from mid-August until September 15, 1918.

The gaudily painted in the form of a fish was this F.2B, B1288, circa 1918.

It was inevitable that an aeroplane, which had given such convincing proof of its fighting ability, should be selected for Home Defence duties. The choice was hastened by the beginning of the night raids on London in September 1917. The intention was that nine squadron of the 6th Brigade were to be equipped with Bristol Fighters. These were Squadrons Nos. 33, 36, 38, 39, 51, 75, 76, 77 and 141. Only Nos. 36, 39 and 141 were fully equipped with the type, and Nos. 33 and 76 had a few.

Some of the Home Defence Bristol Fighters had an unusual system of gun sighting. The observer's Lewis gun was sighted by the pilot by means of a special sight mounted on the centre-section and inclined upwards and forwards at an angle of 45 degrees. The observer aligned his gun parallel to the sight, the pilot manoeuvred the aircraft until he had lined up the sights on the target, whereupon he signalled to the observer, who opened fire.

Just before the advent of the Bristol F.2A, Sergeant A.E.Hutton of No. 39 Squadron had invented a special illuminated gun-sight for use at night. The Hutton sight was in use from March 1917, until the following December, when it was superseded by the Neame sight, which was illuminated in similar fashion to the Hutton Sight.

The night-flying Bristols accounted for two of the thirty-eight Gothas which, in company with three Zeppelin Giants and two single-engined machines, made the last aeroplane attack on London on the night of may 19th/20th, 1918. Fourteen of the eighty-four Home Defence aircraft which

The Shark Tooth design was not restricted to the fighters of World War Two as this F.2 fighter, C4879, reveals.

took off to attack the German force were Bristol Fighters. Lieutenant E.E.Turner and Air Mechanic H.B.Barwise of No. 141 Squadron attacked a Gotha which had survived the attack of Major F.Sowrey of No. 143 (Camel) Squadron. The Gotha pilot had been wounded by Major Sowrey and the further damage inflicted by the Bristol forced the German machine down. It tried to land at Harrietsham aerodrome but crashed.

The Bristol Fighter shared with the S.E.5a a certain disadvantage for night work, both machines had stationary water-cooled engines which took longer to warm up than the contemporary rotary motors, and both had long noses which made them comparatively difficult to land at night on small aerodromes. At the time of the Armistice at least one mixed squadron of

F.2B, F4717, of No. 2 Squadron which was to be converted to a Mk.IV.

Bristol Fighters and Sopwith Pups was due to be re-equipped with the single-seat fighter version of the Avro 504K.

The United States of America entered the war on April 6, 1917, and set about the production of aircraft on a characteristically ambitious scale. The initial 'Procurement Program' planned for the immediate acquisition of 7,375 aircraft, and the ultimate aim was the production of no fewer than 20,475 machines in twelve months. A substantial number of these aircraft were of British design. Towards the end of 1917 it was arranged that the Bristol Fighter would be produced by the Curtiss Aeroplane and Motor Corporation, and 2,000 were ordered. Two Bristol-built airframes were sent as samples to the Curtiss works.

The Curtiss-built machines were to have had the 300-hp Wright-built

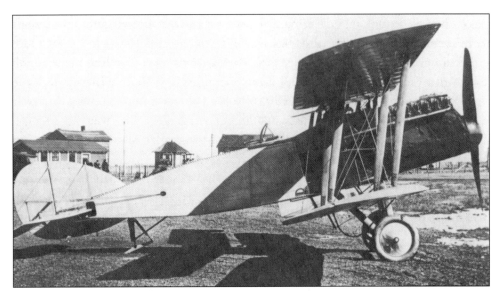

Curtiss-built USA-0-1 with Liberty engine.

Hispano-Suiza engine, but political pressure was brought to bear in favour of the American Liberty 12, which was substituted for the Wright-Hispano. This was done in defiance of the strenuous opposition of the British & Colonial Aeroplane Co., for Captain Barnwell knew that the Liberty was too bulky and too heavy for the aeroplane.

Responsibility for the engineering behind the production of the Liberty-powered Bristol Fighter rested with the U.S. Government until the production programme was well advanced. Even when the Government relinquished that responsibility, the Curtiss Company were not allowed to

The first American US-XB-1A in 1918 with semi-moncoque fuselage at McCook field.

make changes of any magnitude. At an early stage, Curtiss engineers realised that Barnwell was correct in thinking that the installation of the Liberty engine in the Bristol Fighter would not be satisfactory, they therefore began to design a completely new aircraft (the Curtiss CB) to use the Liberty and to perform the same duties as the Bristol.

The installation of the Liberty engine in the Bristol Fighter was clumsy, the

Bristol F.2Bs of No.. 139 Squadron, Italy, 1915.

radiators were badly placed, and the aeroplane, nose-heavy, was thoroughly unpleasant to fly. The first machine was completed in March, 1918, and was delivered to the U.S. Air Service during the following month. Twenty-seven were built before production was halted and the remainder of the contract cancelled. Blind to their own blunder in fitting the Liberty to an aeroplane unsuited to the engine, the U.S. Army shifted the blame on to the innocent aircraft and condemned the Bristol Fighter as dangerous.

Another version of the design was, however, ordered in large quantities in America. The Engineering Division of the Bureau of Aircraft Production undertook the fairly extensive re-design of the Bristol Fighter and evolved two designs, both for aircraft which had completely re-designed structures: one version was powered by the 300-hp Hispano-Suiza, and was designated

Bristol Type Tourer was based upon the F.2 design. G-EAXA was built in May 1921 and converted to the Type 81 standards with Puma engine.

USB-1, the other was designed for the 290-hp Liberty 8, and was designated USB-2. An optimistic order for 2,000 machines of the USB type was placed.

These aircraft had a veneer-covered fuselage of faired contours, and the area of the vertical tail assembly was increased. Many other detail modifications were made, and the equipment of the machines was different from that of the standard British-made Bristol F.2B.

Some standard Bristol Fighter airframes had been sent to America for experimental purposes. One was fitted with a 300-hp Hispano-Suiza, and had the McCook Field Project No. P.30, a second had one of the first eight-cylinder Liberty 8 engines of 290-hp and the Project No. 37. The latter Bristol crashed before performance tests were carried out. These two Bristol Fighters have been referred to as the USB-1 and USB-2 respectively, but that is incorrect.

F4435, No. 208 Squadron, over Ismailia, Egypt, 1915.

In the summer of 1918, the construction of twelve Bristol Fighters began at McCook Field. The intention was to built eight machines to the basic Bristol design, four with Hispano-Suiza engines and four with the new and redesigned Liberty 8; and the remaining four were to be structurally similar but with veneer-covered fuselages, two having Hispano-Suiza and two Liberty 8s. Work lagged badly, however, and the construction of the first eight aircraft was finally stopped in September, 1918. Work was still proceeding on the design of the USB-1 and USB-2, which were re-designated USXB-1 and USXB-2 at about this time. A number of fuselages of slightly different design were tested statically, and construction of the two prototypes was begun.

The four Bristol F.2Bs with veneer-covered fuselages were still in hand, but in October, 1918, the construction programme was altered to consist of only two USZB-1s and two USXB-2s were modified to take the 300 -hp Hispano-Suiza, and all four machines emerged in July, 1919, under the designation Engineering Division XB-1A.

The order for 2,000 aircraft of USB type was cancelled at the time of the Armistice, but during 1920 and 1921 forty XB-1As were built by the Dayton-Wright concern. These production machines had the 330-hp Wright H engine, and their all-up weight was about 800lb. greater than that of the original XB-1A. In 1921, one of the production XB-1As was fitted with the 350-hp Packard 1A-1237 engine; and another (A.S.64156) was used as a test-bed for the Curtiss D-12.

FR4582 of No.208 Squadron.

The Bristol Fighter remained in service with the R.A.F. for many years after the Armistice; in fact, it was not retired until 1932. In the post-war years the Bristol was used on Army Co-operation duties by nine Service squadrons, and did yeoman service on the north-west Frontier of India and in Iraq.

Production for the R.A.F. continued until 1926, and the type was used in a large number of experiments with wings of varying aspect ratio, different aerofoil sections, control surfaces, evaporative cooling systems and Handley Page slots. This last device prolonged the Bristol's service life by a few years, and the ultimate Service version had slots, long-travel undercarriage, and a balanced rudder.

Other nations were quick to adopt the type for their air services, and the post-war years saw considerable numbers of variously powered Bristol Fighters bound for destinations in Spain, Belgium, Mexico, Norway, Sweden, Greece, Bulgaria, and the Irish Free State.

A substantial number of Bristol Fighters were given registrations on the British Civil Register, however, many were also shipped abroad. The Bristol Company produced a number of passenger-carrying conversions, and development continued for many years and in many forms.

Bristol F.2A & F.2B Specifications

Production Measurements

Wing span:	39 ft 3 in. (11.96 m)
Wing Area:	405.6 sq. ft (37.68 sq. m)
Chord:	5 ft 6 in.
Wing stagger:	(F.2A) 17.1 in.
	(F.2B) 16.9 in.
Tailplane span:	(F.2A) 12 ft 0 in.
	(F.2B) 12 ft 10 in.
Length:	(F.2A) 26 ft 3 in.
	(F.2B) 26 ft 2 in.

Weights (These varied but examples are quoted.)
F2A production, tare 1717 lbs. maximum loaded 2473 lbs.
F2B production tare (300-hp Hispano-Suiza) 2067 lbs.
Maximum loaded 3020 lbs.

Bristol F.2A & F.2B Specifications

Prototype Measurements

Wing span:	39 ft 2¹/₂ in. (11.94m)
Wing Area:	389 sq. ft (36.14 sq. m)
Chord:	5 ft 6 in.
Wing stagger:	17.1 in.
Tailplane span:	12 ft 0 in.
Length:	25 ft 9 in.
Height:	9 ft 4 in.

Performance

Maximum speed @ S/L (f2A prototype) 110mph. @ 5000ft 106mph. @ 15,000ft 96mph. The fastest model was the F2B (Falcon III) at 115mph @ 9000ft. Climb rate varied with engine and load. Service ceiling from 14,500ft. (F2A prototype) to 20,500ft (290-hp) Siddeley Puma

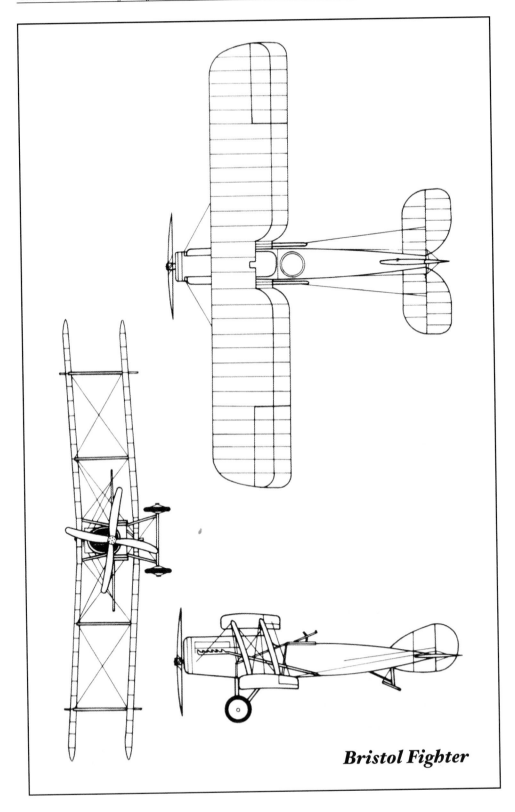

Bristol Fighter

CHAPTER TWO

Albatros Fighters

The *Albatros Werke* produced their first aircraft in 1912, the Albatros L.3, a single-seat scout type. This was followed by the L.9, a single-seat scout type designed by Claude Dornier, but it was the design of the B-series that was to bring the *Albatros Werke* into the forefront of German aviation.

Albatros B-Series

The first of the two-seater reconnaissance/trainers, the B.I, appeared in 1913. The aircraft was initially used as a trainer, but with the outbreak of war it was used both as a trainer and reconnaissance aircraft. Powered by a 100-hp Mercedes D.I and later by the Mercedes D.II engine, with its distinctive `chimney exhaust' manifold, the B.I had a top speed of 65 mph and a duration of 4 hours. It had a wingspan of 47 ft 6 in., a fuselage length of 28 ft 2 in. and a height of 10 ft 4 in. The B.I also had large triangular tail surfaces which also appeared later in the C.I model. These tail surfaces, and the unbalanced rudder and elevator control surfaces, were constructed of a light gauge welded steel-tube and covered in doped fabric.

The wings were of conventional construction, the upper wing being slightly

Albatros B.I showing its wire wheels.

longer than the lower. The aileron operating cables ran along the surface of the lower wing over pulleys close to the rear of the outer, interplane struts.

Only a small number of the aircraft were built before being replaced by the B.II. The B.II, like the B.I, had an extremely strong slab-sided fuselage made up of four spruce longerons and covered with plywood. Like all early aircraft the pilot sat in the rear cockpit, which gave him a very limited view for take-off and landing.

Excellent shot of an Albatros B.II. in flight. The photograph was taken from an accomanying B.II.

Leutnant *von Lauff and* Leutnant *Wilhelm Allmenröder seated in their Albatros B.II.*

The B.II had a wingspan of 42 ft, a fuselage length of 25 ft, and height of 10 ft 4 in. Later the airframe of the B.II was strengthened and a 120-hp Argus As II engine installed. The wingspan was increased to 42 ft 7 in., although all other specifications remained the same with the aircraft designated the B.IIa. Used for training and reconnaissance duties, the B.II and B.IIa were replaced by the B.III with only minor modifications.

The B.III was of the same construction and design as the B.II, although it did have the new tail surfaces that were to become an integral part of the Albatros C.III. It had a smaller wingspan of 36 ft 1 in. and a fuselage length of 25 ft 8 in. Only a small number of this aircraft were built and used for scouting and reconnaissance purposes.

Albatros G.II twin-engined bi-plane standing outside the Linke-Hoffman Works.

Early in 1915 the company embarked on a singularly ambitious project, a four-engined bomber. Designed by Konstr. Grohmann, the Albatros G.I as it was known had a wingspan of 89 ft 7 in. (27 metres), a wing area of 1,485 sq. ft. (138 sq. metres) and a fuselage length of 39 ft 5 in (12 metres). It was indeed a very large aircraft. On the lower wing, four 120-hp Mercedes D.II engines in their

Albatros G.III fresh from the factory.

nacelles were mounted driving four tractor propellers. The first flight took place on January 31, 1916 and was flown by a Swiss pilot named Alexander Hipleh. The G.I became the forerunner of the G.II and G.III although the two latter aircraft were twin-engined bombers.

Albatros C - Series

With the B-series quickly being overtaken by other reconnaissance aircraft, the *Albatros Werke* came up with the two-seater Albatros C.I. It was designed to accommodate the new engines that were now appearing from Mercedes and Benz. The design was based upon that of the B-type using a fuselage that was constructed of four main spruce longerons to which the slab-sided plywood was fixed. The wings were made of wood, but the triangular tail surfaces and ailerons were constructed of a fabric-covered light gauge steel-tube. The undercarriage was of the normal 'V'-type design of hollow wooden fairings and steel tube Fitted in the centre of the axle, was a `claw' type brake which was operated by means of a lever in the cockpit. It worked well most of the time, but problems did arise when the claw ran into a tree stump causing the aircraft to invariably end up on its nose.

The C.I had a wingspan of 42 ft 4 in., a fuselage length of 25 ft 9 in. and a height of 10 ft 4 in. Powered by a 150-hp Benz Bz III/ 160-hp Mercedes D III/ 180-hp Argus As III engines which gave the aircraft speeds of between 85 - 105 mph depending on which engine was used. The engine, which was mounted on wooden bearers had a 'chimney' style exhaust manifold which projected the exhaust gases over the top of the upper wing. The radiators were positioned either side of the fuselage and were of the type that could be enlarge depending on the conditions in the different theatres of operations in which the aircraft

Anthony Fokker demonstrating the synchronised machine gun to the military. The wooden disc shown mounted on the spinner showed the position of the line of fire.

was active.

One of the first sections to receive the aircraft was the *Feldfliegerabteilungen*, where it was used extensively for artillery spotting and photo-reconnaissance missions. A number of Germany's top fighter pilots cut their teeth on the Albatros C.I, among them Manfred von Richthofen and Oswald Boelcke. A C.Ia version was also introduced some months later with a revised radiator system but only a few of this type were built.

Armed with a manually operated Parabellum machine-gun in the observers cockpit and a fixed, forward firing synchronised Spandau machine-gun, the C.I was also capable of carrying a small number of bombs in a vertical drum-shaped container fitted between the front and rear cockpits.

Vizefeldwebel *Paul; Piechl of* Feldflieger-Abteilung *7b with an Albatros C.I.*

A dual-control trainer was built later and given the designation of Albatros C.Ib.

The arrival of improved Allied fighter aircraft prompted the development of a faster reconnaissance aircraft. Albatros produced the (OAW *Ostdeutsche Albatroswerke*) C.I powered by the 150-hp Benz engine, but only two were built. A second Albatros, the (OAW) C.II built in 1916, powered by a straight eight Mercedes D.IV engine was produced, this time only one was built.

A completely different design early in 1916, produced the Albatros C.II. Called the *Gitterschwanz* (Trellis-tail), the design was of the pusher type looking very similar to the de Havilland D.H.2. Powered by a 150-hp Benz Bz.III engine, the C.II did not measure up to expectations and only one was built. This was quickly followed by the Albatros C.IV which reverted back to the original basic design. A 160-hp Mercedes D.III engine was fitted into the C.III fuselage to which a C.II assembly and undercarriage were fixed. Again only one of these aircraft was made.

Again another single experimental aircraft appeared in 1915, with the arrival of the Albatros C.IV. It was in reality almost a C.III inasmuch as it utilised the fuselage, tail assembly and complete undercarriage of the aircraft. The wings however were deep-sectioned and special interplane struts which dispensed with the need for incidence bracing. The pilot's cockpit reverted back to the original position where the pilot sat in the rear section of the fuselage.

Albatros C.III fighter.

A purely experimental model, the Albatros C.V Experimental, was built at the beginning of 1916. With a wing span of 42 ft supported by 'I' struts in an effort to test the interplane bracing. Powered by an eight-cylinder 220-hp Mercedes D.IV engine, the CV Experimental supplied a great deal of information to *Albatros Werke*. The C.VI followed soon afterwards and was based on the C.III airframe and powered by a 180-hp Argus As.III engine giving the aircraft a top speed of 90 mph whilst carrying enough fuel for a 4$^{1}/_{2}$ hours flight duration. The wingspan of 38 ft 5 in. and fuselage length of 25 ft 11 in., made this model smaller that its predecessor making it slightly lighter and faster.

In 1917 a night bomber version, the C.VIII (N), evolved. Bombs were carried beneath the lower wings, but it was only powered by a 160-hp Mercedes D.III engine. Only one was built. This aircraft had a considerably larger wingspan than the other models - 54 ft 11 in. Although the fuselage length was only 24 ft 1 in. slightly smaller than previous models.

At the same time as the night bomber was being constructed, a two-seat fighter/reconnaissance aircraft the Albatros C.IX, was being built. With a straight lower wing and a considerably swept upper wing it presented an unusual aircraft, but only three were built. It had a wingspan of 34 ft 2 in., a fuselage length of 27ft. and a top speed of 97 mph. It is said that one of these aircraft was given to Manfred von Richthofen as his personal transport.

This was followed by the Albatros C.X of which a large number were built

Rare and unusual shot of an Albatros C.III on patrol over the Belgian Front.

and by four sub-contractors. Very similar in design to the previous models its role was primarily for reconnaissance work. Its successor however, the C.XII, was an extremely elegant looking two-seat fighter and was armed with manually operated Parabellum machine-gun and one fixed, forward-firing synchronised Spandau machine-gun. The fuselage flowed from the horizontal knife-edge at the rear of the aircraft to the large spinner airscrew in the nose in one flowing shape. The wings and undercarriage were same as the C.X. The C.XII had a wingspan of 47 ft 2 in., a fuselage length of 29 ft 1 in., a height of 10 ft 8 in. and a top speed of 103 mph.

The Albatros C.XIII was again solely for experimental purposes with only one being built. It was an extremely elegant looking two-seat fighter and was armed with manually operated Parabellum machine-gun and one fixed, forward-firing synchronised Spandau machine-gun. It had a wingspan of 32 ft 10 in., a fuselage length of 25 ft 7 in., a height of 8 ft 11 in. and a top speed of 103 mph.

A return to the original design of the two-seater reconnaissance produced

Albatros C.XII

the Albatros C.XIV. There was one difference, and that was that the C.XIV had staggered wings and again only one was built. With a wingspan of 34 ft 12 in., a fuselage length of 22 ft 8 in. and a height of 8 ft 11 in., the C.XIV was powered by a 220-hp Benz IVa engine and had a top speed of 103 mph. The C.XIV was later modified into the C.XV, the wingspan increased to 38 ft 6 in. and the fuselage length to 24 ft 6 in. It had a top speed of 103 mph and was armed with one Parabellum machine-gun in the rear cockpit and a forward firing synchronised Spandau machine-gun in front of the pilot. Although the aircraft was put into immediate production, it was too late for it to appear as the end of the war came before the first completed model came off the production line.

The air supremacy of the Imperial German Air Force during 1916, had been gradually eroded by the rapid development of the Allied fighter aircraft. In a

Albatros CIII

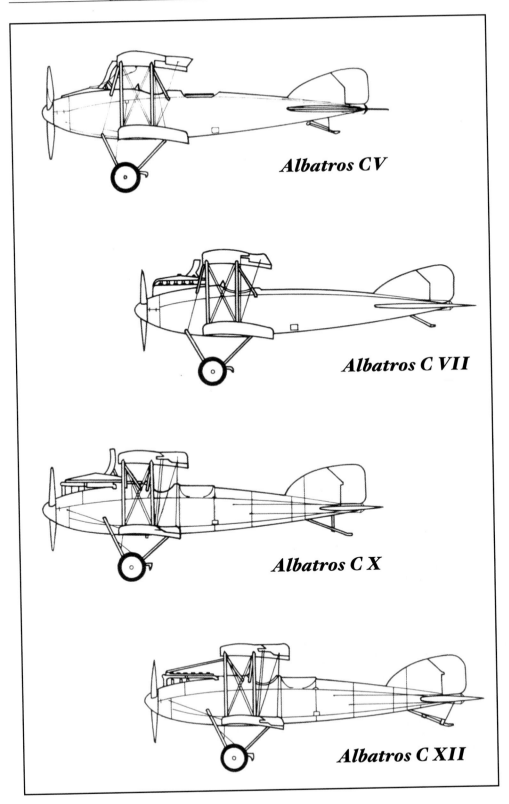

Albatros CV

Albatros C VII

Albatros C X

Albatros C XII

desperate attempt to gain control again, the *Albatros Werke* was approached to design and build a fighter that would do just that. Looking at the highly manoeuvrable Nieuport that was causing some of the problems, the company's top designer Robert Thelen set to work and produced a design that combined speed and firepower. If his aircraft couldn't out-manoeuvre the Nieuport he would catch it and blast it out of the sky and that is precisely what he did when he designed and built the Albatros D-series

Albatros D-series

The first of the Albatros D-series, the D.I, was designed by *Dipl. Ing.* Robert Thelen, *Dipl. Ing.* Schubert and *Ing.* Gnaedig. It was powered by a 160-hp Mercedes engine or the 150-hp Benz, which was enclosed in a semi-monocoque plywood fuselage. The cylinder heads and valve gear were left exposed, as this gave assisted cooling and greater ease of access for the engineers who had to work on the engine. Engine cooling was achieved by mounting two Windoff radiators, one on each side of the fuselage and between the wings, and a slim water tank mounted above the and toward the rear of the engine at an offset angle to port. The extra power given to the aircraft enabled the firepower, twin fixed Spandau machine guns, to be increased without loss of performance.

The fuselage consisted of thick plywood formers and six spruce longerons. Screwed to this frame were plywood panels and the engine was installed with easily removable metal panels for both protection and ease of maintenance.

A captured Albatros D..I in R.F.C. markings belonging to Leutnant *Büttner after he was forced to land. This gave the Allies an excellent opportunity to thoroughly examine this fighter.*

The upper and lower wings, and the tail surfaces, were covered with doped fabric. The fixed tail surfaces, upper and lower fins, were made of plywood. The control surfaces were fabric covered over a welded steel-tube frame with a small triangular balance portion incorporated in the rudder and the one-piece elevator. Control of the surfaces was by means of the conventional control column and rudder bar. The control column had an elevator locking device fitted along with the triggers that operated the twin fixed synchronised Spandau machine-guns.

The wings of the Albatros D.I were unequal, inasmuch as the upper wing was built in one piece, whilst the lower wing was constructed in two halves. Built round two main spruce spars with plywood ribs and internal wire bracing, they were covered in doped fabric. The steel-framed ailerons were operated by steel cables which ran down an arm that was fixed mid-span on the aileron, through the lower wing to the control column.

The undercarriage was of a conventional streamlined steel-tube construction, and the vee-type chassis was fixed to the fuselage by means of sockets and sprung through the wheels with rubber shock cord. The spoked wheels were invariably enclosed in canvas, and some of the later models actually had mudguards fitted.

The D.I. was a very satisfactory aircraft to fly, but it was discovered to have a major drawback during combat. The top wing, because of its position to the fuselage, obscured the pilot's forward field of vision. The problem was solved by cutting out a semi-circular section of the top wing in front of the pilot, and by

Albatros D.I taxiing out to go on patrol. The pilot is Prince Friedrich Karl of Prussia. Shortly after this photograph was taken he was shot down and wounded by Lieutenant Pickthorn of No. 32 Squadron RFC.

lowering the wing so that the pilot could see over the top.

The first operational unit to receive the Albatros D.I. was *Jasta* 2 on September 17, 1916, and commanded by the legendary Oswald Boelcke. Three weeks later Boelcke was killed when his Albatros D.I. was in involved in a mid-air collision with his wingman Erwin Böhme as they both dived into attack the same British aircraft, a D.H.2 of No. 24 Squadron R.F.C. As more and more D.Is were produced and assigned to front-line *Jastas*, they replaced the already outdated Fokker D.IIIs and Halberstadts.

Although the D.I. was not built in any great numbers, when compared to

New Albatros D.Is arrive at Jagdstaffel *2 in 1916.*

later D-series models, by November 1916 over fifty of the aircraft had seen service on the Western Front. The potential of the aircraft was soon realised and the design of the aircraft allowed room for improvement.

In the middle of 1916 the German Naval High Command decided that it would be a good idea to have a single-seat fighter floatplane (*Jagdeinsitzer Wasser*) as a defence aircraft. The Albatros D.I. was used as the basis of the Albatros W.4 although the latter was considerably larger in overall dimensions. The wing span was increased by 3 ft 3 in. and although the profile remained much the same, much longer and stronger centre-section struts were required.

The W.4 was powered by a six-cylinder, in-line, water-cooled 160-hp Mercedes D.III engine, had a top speed of 100 mph and an operating ceiling of 9,840 ft. It could stay on station for about three hours and deal comfortably with any Allied patrol seaplanes that strayed into the area. However the heavily

Albatros W.4 on its tail stand.

armed Felixstowe flying boats from R.N.A.S. Felixstowe and R.N.A.S. Yarmouth, were a different prospect altogether. Not many of the German pilots would attack these aircraft except in the most dire of circumstances. The W.4 was armed with twin fixed forward-firing synchronised Spandau machine-guns, though on occasions only one was fitted. From September 1916 to December 1917, 118 Albatros W.4s were delivered to the German Navy. The Albatros W.1, W.2 and W.3, were all derivatives of models from other series.

The W.1 was an unarmed reconnaissance version of the Albatros B II and was powered by a 150-hp Benz III engine. It had a wingspan of 36 ft 1 in., a fuselage length of 25 ft 8 in. and 18 ft 2 in. floats. Only a small number were built. The W.2 was based of the Albatros C.II and was powered by a 160-hp Mercedes D.III engine. It had a wingspan of 38 ft 5 in., a fuselage length of 26 ft 3 in. and a height of 10 ft 2 in. It had a n operating ceiling of 11,000 feet and a duration of four hours. It was armed initially with a single manually operated Parabellum machine-gun mounted in the rear observers cockpit. The floats were 18 ft 2 in. and only the one model was built.

A single purpose built seaplane was built for the German Navy in July 1916, the Albatros W.3. Designed primarily as a torpedo attack aircraft, it was powered by two 150-hp Benz III pusher engines. It had a wingspan of 74 ft 6 in., a fuselage length of 43 ft and a top speed of 83 mph. Armed with two manually operated Parabellum machine-guns the W.3 also carried a torpedo slung between the 48ft. 6in. floats. Only the one model was built but it became the basis of the W.5.

Albatros D.II

The shortcomings of the Albatros D.I. were resolved with the appearance of the D.II. One of the main criticisms was that the upper wing obscured the pilot's forward and upward vision to some degree. This was solved by retaining the semicircular cut-out in the upper wing, but re-positioning the upper wing by lowering it closer to the fuselage. The trestle-type centre-section cabane was dispensed with and replaced with two sets of out-splayed 'N' centre-section struts. The first D.II models retained the cumbersome radiator system of the D.I but later the installation of a aerofoil-shaped Teeves and Braun radiator system was installed in the starboard side of the upper wing. This addition streamlined the appearance of the aircraft noticeably and pleasantly, to the extent that any warplane bristling with guns could be deemed too pleasant to look at.

The Albatros D.II was assigned to *Jasta* 2 among others, and it was in one of these, No. 491/16, Manfred von Richthofen claimed his first victory, a French Farman S.11, on September 17, 1915. Another pilot, *Prinz* Friedrich Karl von Preussen, who was CO of *Flieger Abteilung* A. 258, a two-seater reconnaissance unit, kept an Albatros D.I at *Jasta* 2 for his personal use in which, between his flight duties, would go on patrol with them in his single-seat fighter. It was in this aircraft that he was shot down and killed on 21 March 1917.

November 1916 saw twenty-eight D.IIs operating on the Western Front, but by January 1917, the number of D.Is had reduced dramatically having been replaced by the D.IIs and the total of D.IIs operating on the Front had reached 214. Late in 1916 the Albatros D.III appeared with subtle, but noticeable changes to the Albatros D.II. But it was to be the middle of 1917 before the

Albatros D.II

Albatros D.II

D.III replaced the D.II in any numbers. Such was the demand for the Albatros D.II, that the L.V.G.- *Luft-Verkehrs Gesellschaft* were licensed to build the aircraft under the designation of L.V.G. D.I.

A young Manfred von Richthofen standing in front of his Albatros D.II.

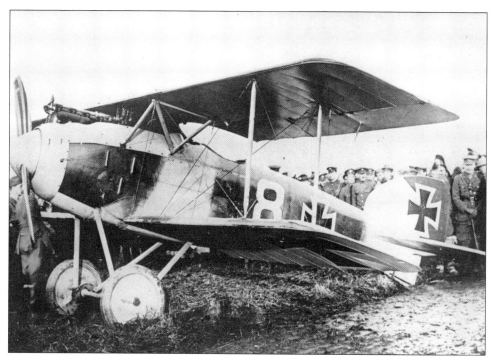

Leutnant *Max Böhme's Albatros D.II of* Jasta 5 *after being brought down by Lieutenant Pearson of No. 29 Squadron, R.F.C. and Lieutenants Graham and Boddy of No. 11 Squadron, R.F.C. Böhme became a PoW.*

Albatros D.I/ D.II Specifications

Performance

Wingspan: Upper 27 ft. 10_ ins. (8.50 m).
Lower: 26 ft. 5 ins. (7.75 m).
Length: 24 ft. 3 ins. (7.40 m).
Height: 9 ft. 6 ins. (2.95 m).
Weight Empty: 1,423 lb. (647 kg).
Weight Loaded: 1,980 lb. (899 kg).
Maximum Speed: 109 mph. (175 km. hr.)
Ceiling: 17.000 ft. (5,180 m)
Duration: $1^{1}/_{2}$ hours.
Armament: Two fixed Spandau machine guns synchronised to fire through the propeller.
Engine: 150-hp Benz Bz III or 160-hp Mercedes 6-cylinder in-line water-cooled engine.

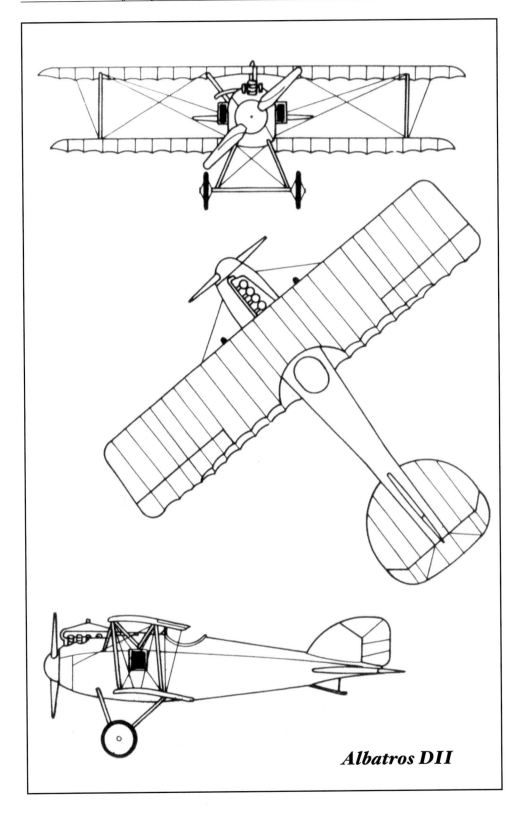

Albatros DII

Leutnant *Karl Schäfer standing in front of his Albatros D.III about to leave on a sortie. His flying clothes can be seen on the port wing.*

Albatros D.III

The design of the D.III to concentrate their design on the pilot's visibility during a combat situation. The capture of a number of Nieuport Scouts earlier in the war had give the German manufacturers a few ideas, which resulted, as far as the Albatros was concerned, in a drastic redesign of the wing arrangement

Albatros D.III fighters of Jasta 4 and 11 at Roucourt. The second aircraft is Manfred von Richthofen'.

using the sesquiplane layout. The upper wingspan was increased and the wingtips rounded instead of the squared off ends of the D.II. The lower wing was constructed on a one piece spruce spar with plywood formers and interplane braced by steel-tube vees. The remainder of the aircraft was constructed as the D.II models.

Initially the aerofoil-shaped radiator was, like previous models, mounted centrally. It was soon realised however, that if that radiator was to be punctured by a bullet during combat, the pilot could, with the precipitation of the slipstream, end up with a stream of scalding water in his face. The radiator was moved toward the starboard side of the centre section.

The arrival of the D.III in the early months of 1917 had an almost immediate impact upon the air war on the Western Front. Known as 'Bloody April', the Albatros D.IIs and D.IIIs wreaked havoc upon the poorly armed B.E.2cs, which

Manfred von Richthofen taking off in his all-red Albatros D.III.

were the R.F.C's mainstay at the time. Manfred von Richthofen's scarlet Albatros D.III, No.789/17, was rapidly adding to his tally of Allied aircraft during this period. *Jagdstaffelns* 1-37 had by the beginning of June been equipped with the D.III in considerable numbers and were making their presence felt. But by the autumn the tide was starting to turn in favour of the Allies. The superiority of the Albatros IIIs however was short-lived with the arrival of the Sopwith Triplane and the SPAD S VII, and a little later the S.E.5 and Sopwith Camel, even though there were over 450 Albatros D.IIIs in Front line service in November 1917. The Germans quickly realised that every time they seem to come up with a superior design the Allies countered it with an even better one. The Allies also had the advantage of being able to turn to a variety of aircraft manufacturers, whereas the Germans were limited in their choice.

Carl Schäfer in the cockpit of his Albatros D.III.

The Albatros W.5 seaplane was one of the largest seaplanes of its time appeared in May 1917. Five of these aircraft were produced for the German Navy between May 1917 and January 1918, and although said to have been based on the W.3, it looked markedly different. It was powered by two 150-hp Benz III pusher engines which gave it a top speed of 83 mph and patrol duration of four hours. It was armed with two manually operated Parabellum machine-guns and a torpedo, that was housed so well into the underside of the fuselage, that only the bottom rear fin and part of the rounded nose showed beneath the shaped line of the fuselage. The vertical surfaces of the aircraft were of a triangular shape, whilst the 74 ft 6 in. wings were swept slightly back and had four ailerons fitted. It had a fuselage length of 43 ft and had a height of 14 ft.

By the summer of 1917, the D.III had been superseded by the Albatros D.V. and D.Va although it was to be toward the end of the year before it went into service with the *Jastas*. The D.V arrived just as the S.E.5s and SPADs (*Société Pour Aviation et ses Dériéves*) and Sopwith Camels of the Allies, started to regain control of the skies. The same problem seemed to dog Albatros aircraft throughout its development, and that was that the lower wing had a tendency to break up in a prolonged dive. In one incident, *Vfzw.* Festnter of *Jasta* 11 carried out a test flight in an Albatros D.III, at 13,000 feet the port lower wing broke up and it was only his experience and a great deal of luck, that prevented the aircraft crashing into the ground. Even the legendary Manfred *Freiherr* von Richthofen experienced a similar incident on January 24, 1917, while testing one

Leutnant *Karl Allmenröders Albatros D.III of* Jasta 11.

Albatros D.IIIs of Jasta 11 *at Roucourt - April 1917.*

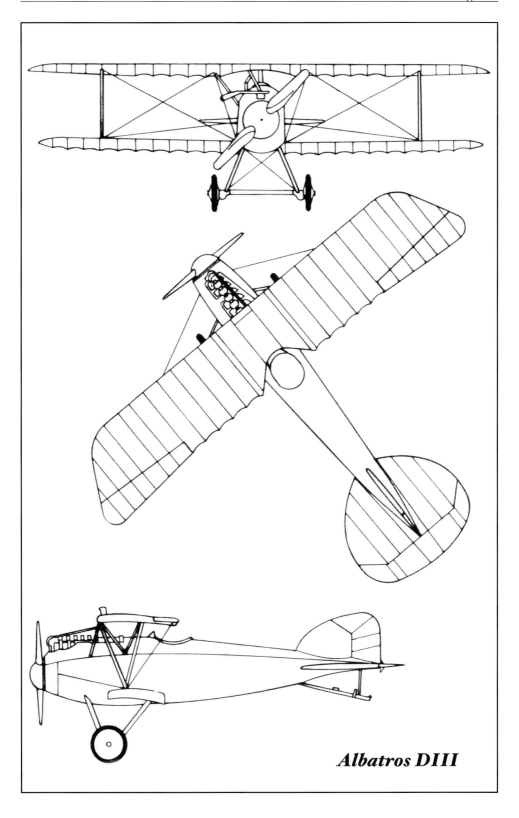

Albatros DIII

of the new Albatros D.IIIs that had recently arrived at *Jasta* 11.

Tests were carried out and it was discovered that the single spar was positioned too far aft causing vibrations which increased as the dive continued. This eventually resulted in the structure of the wing collapsing under the erratic movement. A temporary stopgap was achieved by fitting a short strut from the vee interplane to the leading edge. Instructions were then given to pilots not to carry out long dives

Manfred von Richthofen in his flight gear standing by his aircraft after arriving for a visit to an unknown Jasta.

in the Albatros D.III, which as one can imagine drastically reduce the faith the pilots had in the aircraft especially when under combat conditions.

Albatros D.IV

The design teams in the *Albatros Werke* were not being idle, whilst the Albatros D.V was being developed, an experimental model the D.IV was produced. A prototype was developed, the Albatros D.IV, which designer Robert Thelen hoped would supersede the D.III and help regain control of the skies above the Western Front. News from the Front concerning the arrival of the S.E.5 and Sopwith aircraft and their performances, pressurised Thelen into re-thinking his projected performance figures. He reverted back to the original design of the D.I of a two-spar lower wing with parallel interplane struts. With the fuselage of a D.Va and the wings of a D.II, the experimental fighter was powered by a specially geared version of the 160-hp Mercedes D.III engine, which allowed the engine to be completely enclosed in the nose. A headrest was fitted, and together with a curved trailing edge, gave the aircraft a racy streamlined look. Although adding to the racy line of the aircraft, the headrest was removed before combat mission because it restricted the pilot's rearward vision. Unfortunately although the Albatros D.IV looked the part, its performance did not match it, and only the one model was built. There were a number of insurmountable problems with the engine and the project was scrapped.

The *Albatros Werke* was pressurised into improving the Albatros with the result that the Albatros D.V was developed. The D.V had a major change to the shape of the fuselage, The D.III fuselage, with its flat sides, was replaced with an elliptical fuselage. The sesquiplane wing layout was fitted to the new fuselage, whilst the vertical tail unit was very similar to that used on the D.III. The gap between the upper wings and the fuselage of the D.V was reduced considerably, which meant that stubs had to be built into the belly of the aircraft to which the lower wing was attached. This in essence meant that the gap between the wings

Oberleutnant *Eduard Ritter von Schleich on September 21, 1917, after his 20th victory for which he was awarded the* Orden Pour le Mérite. *He stands in front of his Albatros D.Va and shows his personal insignia.*

stayed the same as those of the D.III. The aileron control system was also redesigned, as up to this point the operating cables were run from the aileron crank into the lower wing at a point directly behind the interplane strut, and from there to the fuselage through the wing. The new design channelled the cables through guide chutes up into the upper wing, through the wing and into the fuselage. Only the D.V model was cabled in this fashion, when the D.Va appeared the cables runs reverted back to the original design.

The fuselage was of a semi-monocoque structure consisting of eight spruce longerons and plywood formers, which went from a fully elliptical shape at the nose, to a horizontal knife-edge at the tail. Shaped plywood panels were then pinned and screwed to the structure which was so strong that it required no internal bracing. The tailplane was of wooden construction covered in a doped fabric, the round-shaped rudder on the other hand was of a light gauge steel-tube construction covered in a doped fabric. There were also two square inspection panels fitted between the tailplane and the fin which gave easy access for maintenance purposes.

Fitted with a 200-hp Mercedes D.IIIa 6-cylinder in-line water-cooled engine, the increased speed of the D.V started to redress some of the balance of air power, but not sufficient enough to make any substantial difference. Even the appearance of the D.Va, although being a slightly superior aircraft to the D.V, did nothing to improve the German air superiority.

Armed with twin fixed forward-firing synchronised Spandau machine-guns, which were fired from twin triggers fixed to the control column. Either gun could be fired independently which helped conserve ammunition when in a prolonged battle.

Albatros D.IV Specifications

Wingspan;	Upper 29 ft 8 ins. (9.05 m).
	Lower 28 ft 6 ins. (8.25 m).
Length;	24 ft 1 ins. (7.33 m).
Height:	9 ft 10 ins. (2.7 m).
Weight Empty:	1,454 lb. (661 kg.).
Weight Loaded:	1,949 lb. (886 kg.).
Maximum speed:	103 mph. (165 km.hr.).
Ceiling:	18,000ft. Duration: 2 hours.

Armament: 2 fixed Spandau machine guns synchronised to fire through the propeller.
Engine: 160-hp Mercedes D.III 6-cylinder in-line water-cooled.

Albatros D.V

The D.Va appeared just one month after the D.V and the only difference between the two, was the re-routing of the aileron control cables back to their original positions. Tests were also carried out to determine the cause of the wing failures that continued to haunt the Albatros. In one incident, *Leutnant* von Hippel of *Jasta 5*, who whilst in a dive in his Albatros D.Va with its black

Albatros D.Va about to take-off. Note the memeber of the ground crew holding down the tail.

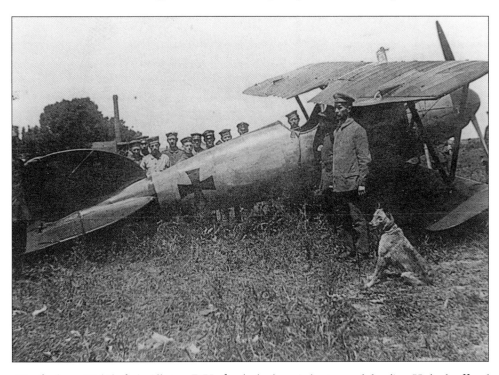

Manfred von Richthofen's Albatros D.V after he had carried out a crash landing. He had suffered a head wound during a dog fight and managed to get his aircraft back to his base. The dog sitting beside the aircraft is said to be Richthofen's dog Moritz.

fire-eating dragon emblazoned along the fuselage, at a height of 16,000 feet, chasing after an Allied aircraft, suddenly discovered to his horror that his lower port wing had become separated from the rest of his aircraft. With tremendous skill and a degree of luck, he managed to crash land the aircraft without

Manfred von Richthofen in the light coloured sweater, on a visit to Jasta Boelcke.

suffering serious injury to himself.

Earlier tests had identified the cause, which was in the positioning of the lower wing spar, the problem was of course was how to solve it. After many trials a small strengthened auxiliary strut was fitted between the interplane struts and the leading edge of the lower wing. A number of dive tests were successfully carried out and with the knowledge that this was a problem that could be cured in the field, a number of auxiliary spars were flown to various *Jastas* so that the modification could be carried out.

A number of Germany's top fighter pilots flew the Albatros D.V, Manfred von Richthofen - The Red Baron, *Hauptmann* Eduard *Ritter* von Schleich - The Black Knight, *Leutnant* Max Müller and *Oberleutnant* Ernst Udet, all of which at some time or another had problems with the aircraft. At the peak of the war in March 1918, over 1,000 Albatros D.V and D.Va models were fighting with 80 *Jastas* at the Front.

Many of Britain's top fighter pilots, including Mick Mannock and James B.

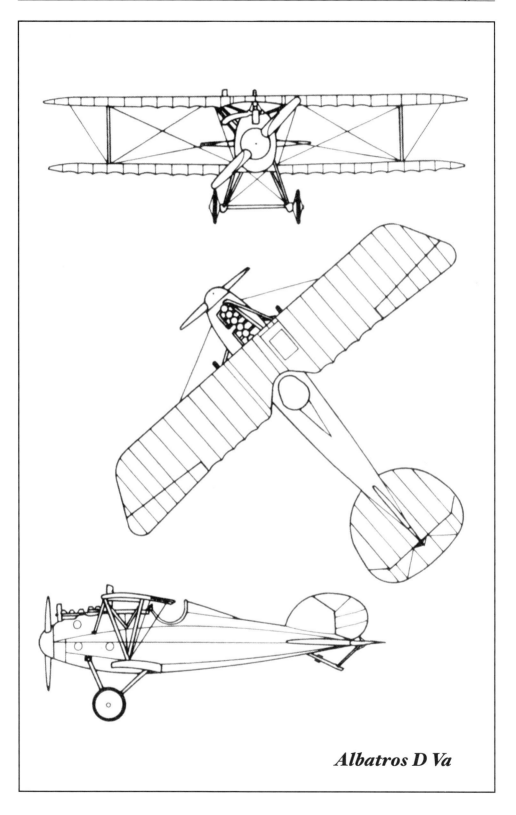

Albatros D Va

McCudden, paid tribute to the agility and firepower of the Albatros D.Vs that they encountered. Numerous accounts stated that after firing bursts of machine-gun fire through these aircraft, they still managed to come back fighting. This was probably just as much a tribute to the pilots as it was to the machine. McCudden remembered fighting one such Albatros D.V with a green tail and a white inverted 'V' across the top of the wing. The two had met twice before and had fought vicious battles, only breaking off to refuel and rearm. Then on the third occasion McCudden managed to get the better of the German and shot him down. Even then, according to McCudden, it was more by luck than judgement.

Albatros D.VII

With the Albatros D.V model being superseded by the Fokker D.III in the D-series trials at Aldershof, the company produced another of their experimental fighters - the Albatros D.VII.

It was of the standard Albatros construction, but with ailerons fitted at all four wingtips linked with a strut. Powered by a V-8 195-hp Benz Bz.IIIb engine which gave it a top speed of 128 mph and a flight duration of two hours, this was the first time a V-8 engine had been used in an Albatros. The D.VII had a wingspan of 30 ft 7 in., a fuselage length of 21 ft 9 in., a height of 8ft 10 in. and was armed with twin fixed forward-firing Spandau machine-guns. Only the one model was Albatros built.

Albatros D.VII Specifications

Wingspan;	Upper 30 ft 7 ins. (9.32 m).
	Lower 28 ft 6 ins. (8.25 m).
Length;	21 ft 9 ins. (7.33 m).
Height:	8 ft 10 ins. (2.7 m).
Weight Empty:	1,386 lb. (630 kg.).
Weight Loaded:	1,947 lb. (885 kg.).
Maximum speed:	127.5 mph. (204 km. hr.).
Ceiling:	20,000 ft (5,700 m)
Duration:	2 hours.
Armament:	2 fixed Spandau machine-guns synchronised to fire through the propeller.
Engine:	195-hp Benz Bz IIIb V-8 6-cylinder in-line water-cooled.

Albatros Dr.I

The appearance of the Albatros Dr.I in 1917 was to assess the possibilities of producing a triplane. After many tests the aircraft was deemed to be no better than the D.V and was not proceeded with. Having said that, at the beginning of 1918 another triplane appeared, the Albatros Dr.II. The heavily staggered triple wings were braced with very wide struts and ailerons were fitted to all the wingtips. Powered by a V-8 195-hp Benz Bz.IVb engine with frontal-type radiators that were mounted in the centre section between the upper and middle wings, the speed of the aircraft was affected considerably because of the drag caused the radiators position.

Albatros Dr.I Specifications

Wingspan;	28 ft 7 ins. (8.7 m).
Length;	24 ft. 0 ins. (7.3 m).
Height:	8 ft 0 ins. (2.42 m).
Weight Empty:	1,386 lb. (630 kg.).
Weight Loaded:	1,947 lb. (885 kg.).
Maximum speed:	108 mph.
Ceiling:	16,000 ft (5,700 m).
Duration:	1 hour.

Armament: 2 fixed Spandau machine guns synchronised to fire through the propeller..
Engine: 160-hp Mercedes D.III, 6-cylinder in-line water-cooled.

Albatros D.VIII

Two months later in August 1917, another experimental fighter appeared, the D.VIII. It was powered by a V-8 195-hp Benz Bz.IIIb engine, which gave the aircraft a top speed of 128 mph and a climb rate of almost 1,000 feet per minute. Again only the one model was built.

A two-seater reconnaissance/bomber appeared at the beginning of 1918, the Albatros J II. Powered by a 220-hp Benz IVa engine which gave the aircraft a top speed of 88 mph, the J.II was armed with twin fixed, downward firing Spandau machine guns and one manually operated Parabellum machine gun in the rear cockpit. The downward firing guns protruded through the floor of the fuselage between the legs of the undercarriage. Four examples were built but it arrived after the Junkers J I and the success of the J.I overshadowed the J II to the extent that no more were built.

A number of prototypes made their appearance early in 1918, the first being the Albatros D IX. It was powered by a 180-hp Mercedes D.IIIa giving it a top speed of 97 mph. Only one was built. A second model appeared, the Albatros D X, powered by a V-8 195-hp Benz IIIb engine. This gave the aircraft a top speed of 106 mph. At a fighter competition at Aldershof, it initially out performed all the other competitors, but was unable to sustain the progress throughout. Again only the one model was built. The Albatros D XI which followed was the first of the Albatros aircraft to use a rotary engine. Fitted with the Siemens-Halske Sh III of 160-hp, it was installed in a horseshoe-shaped cowling with extensions pointing toward the rear. These extensions assisted in the cooling by sucking air through the cowling. Two prototypes were built, one with a four-bladed propeller, the other with a twin-bladed model.

Albatros D.XI on its tail stand.

Two prototype D.XIIs followed both fitted with different engines, but both fitted with a Böhme undercarriage, which for the first time featured compressed-air shock absorbers. Neither aircraft was considered for production.

A final version of the Albatros seaplane made its appearance in June 1918, the Albatros W.8. This was a deviation from the previous seaplane, inasmuch as it was a single-seater fighter developed as a possible successor to the Brandenburg W.12. Only two of the aircraft were supplied to the German Navy the first incorporated the high-set tailplane that was prominent on the Heinkel design.

Unfortunately it did not have the same strong upswept fuselage as the Brandenburg W.12 as was deemed to be to fragile. The second model had a pointed spinner, that being the only difference. Both aircraft had a wingspan of 37 ft 8 in., a fuselage length of 31 ft 6 in. and a height of 11 ft 2 in. Powered by a 195-hp Benz IIIb V-8 engine, the Albatros W.8 had a top speed of 94 mph and was armed with one manually operated Parabellum machine-gun in the observers cockpit and one fixed, forward-firing synchronised Spandau machine-gun.

The Albatros D.V model was the most famous of all the Albatros aircraft and was assigned to various *Jastas* in May 1917 and in an attempt to bolster a flagging morale, pilots were encouraged to emblazon their aircraft in ways that would personalise them. Manfred von Richthofen had his Albatros D.V, 1177/17, painted a scarlet red as was his later version, 4693/17. Eduard *Ritter* von Schleich had his Albatros D.V painted all black and became known as the `BLACK KNIGHT'. By May 1918 there were 131 Albatros D.Vs and 928 D.Vas in operational service, but by now it was too late the war was over.

But that wasn't the end of service as far as the Albatros was concerned. The end of the war in Europe only served to highlight the civil war that was raging in Russia. A number of Allied pilots had been coerced into fighting for the White Russian forces against the revolutionists, and among them were a number of American pilots who, together with Polish pilots, formed the 7th (*Kosciuszko*) Squadron. The volunteers came under the command of Captain

Believed to be the prototype Albatros D.V.

Merian Cooper, who later found fame as a Hollywood film director, amongst his films was the famous classic `King Kong'. His involvement had come about whilst he had been carrying out relief work in Poland at a time when the country was fighting against, firstly Ukrainian forces and then Soviet forces in an effort to retain their independence.

The Americans found to their surprise, that aircraft assigned to their squadron consisted of Austrian-built Albatros D.IIIs, the very aircraft they had been fighting against only a few months previously. The squadron was formed into two flights, No. 1 and No. 2 and were distinctive in that the noses of the aircraft were red and blue respectively. The Americans were dissatisfied with the rate of fire from the twin fixed, forward-firing Spandau machine-gun and one of the pilots, Lieutenant E.W. Chess, doubled the firing rate of the guns by altering the operating gear. Bomb racks were also devised to enable the aircraft to carry two small bombs after it was realised that their was virtually no aerial opposition and attacks were going to be limited to strafing and low-level bombing runs. The Albatros stayed in service until withdrawn in 1920, by which time the civil unrest in Russia was over.

CHAPTER TWO

Nieuport Scouts

One of the most famous aircraft of the First World War was the French Nieuport. This relatively small aircraft company started life in 1906 as a manufacturer of engine parts and was the brainchild of Édouard de Niéport.

Born in 1875 at Blida, Algeria, de Niéport showed an unusually inquiring interest in the new field of electricity and in speed at a very early age. He started cycle racing relatively successfully in his early twenties, and so as not to embarrass his middle-class parents in this dangerous sport, he changed his name when entering the events to *Nieuport*. In his early thirties he purchased a small workshop in the rue de Seine at Surésnes and started to manufacture his own magnetos and starter motors.

For the next three years he designed and built magnetos and starter motors for the engines of a number of different aircraft companies. Then, in 1909, Niéport decided to build his own aircraft engine and, in order to test it, designed and built his own aircraft. That same year saw the birth of his new aviation company, *Société Anonyme des Établissments Nieuport*.

The first aircraft was a monoplane of simple design and streamlined in such a way that only the head and part of the shoulders of the pilot protruded above the fuselage. The curved shape of the cockpit, in front of the pilot, was raised so as to deflect the wind away from his face. Designated the Nieuport 1, it was powered, initially, by a 20-hp Darracq engine but was shortly to be replaced by a new custom-built Darracq designed by Niéport himself. However, before the engine could be completed the airframe was destroyed in a flood.

Not to be discouraged, Niéport designed and built his second engine, a twin-cylinder 28-hp model that was to be fitted into his second aircraft the Nieuport 2N. Based on the design of the Nieuport 1, it was a sleek monoplane built with four ash longerons covered in doped fabric. The aircraft was tested at the laboratory of the French engineer Gustav Eiffel — the constructor of the Eiffel Tower. The first flight of the Nieuport 2N was on January 5, 1910, and was a complete success. Further trials with a 30-hp Anzani engine were carried out in 1911, but in the same year Édouard Niéport was killed in an air crash. He had been demonstrating his Nieuport 2N at a military exercise at Charny when he was caught in a violent storm and crashed. He died later in hospital at Verdun of his injuries. His brother, Charles Niéport, took over the company almost immediately and continued to develop not only the engines but also the aircraft.

On the January 22, 1912, Charles Niéport gained his pilot's licence and continued to test and demonstrate the company's aircraft. Then, on the January 24, 1913, while demonstrating one of his aircraft at a meeting at Étampes, he too crashed killing himself and his mechanic.

Despite the loss of its two founder members, the company continued to develop the aircraft side of the business using engines manufactured by other companies. The arrival of Gustave Delage at the beginning of 1914 heralded the start of a new era. At the beginning of the First World War the company already had one of their aircraft in use in Turkey. They had been using Nieuport Nie 6 floatplanes for reconnaissance purposes but, with the escalation of the war in Europe, Delage designed and produced the Nieuport Nie 10.

Nieuport Nie. 10 & 12

The Nieuport 10 was a tractor biplane with many similarities to the monoplanes produced by Nieuport before the war. It was a two-seater and appeared in two types, the 10AV (AV signified *avant,* or in front, the position the observer took to the pilot). The other aircraft being the 10AR, in this case *arrière* or behind the pilot.

The *Aviation Militaire* gave its approval and the first production of 10A.2s were delivered to squadrons in the summer of 1915. Although these newly produced aircraft went to observation squadrons within a few months many of them were adapted to single-seat 10C.1s as a stop-gap for fighter operations. To allow these aircraft to operate as 'fighters' a very basic conversion was carried out with the front seat being covered over and a Lewis machine-gun mounted on the top wing and angled upward to fire over the propeller. The two-seaters had their machine-gun mounted in similar fashion but a cut-out in the top wing allowed the observer, in the front seat, to stand and fire. The Nieuport 10 was also used by the Italian Air Force and a number were built in Italy by the Macchi company. Belgian and British squadrons were also equipped with a limited number of the 10A.2.

The Nieuport 10 was fitted with a 80-hp Le Rhône rotary engine, although some had the similarly horse-powered Gnôme or Anzani engines. Carrying two crew members the aircraft's speed was greatly hampered but, in its original observation rôle, this was not considered a drawback.

At this stage of the war, however, there was an increasing need for 'fighters' or 'scouts'. With this in mind Delage, using the basic design of the

10AR, incorporated a 110-hp and 130-hp Clerget 9B rotary engine. This increased engine size necessitated the slight enlargement of the basic Nieuport 10 configuration and the result was designated the Nieuport Nie. 12. Consideration was also given to improving the aircraft's manoeuvrability and general performance as well as increasing the crew's field of vision and firing.

The original armament for the Nieuport 12 was similar to that of the 10 but, with the advance of synchronised gearing, a forward-firing machine-gun

Nieuport 12

was added for the pilot. In 1916 the 'horse-shoe' cowling, that covered the engine, was replaced by a fully circular one, thus causing some confusion when trying to identify types from early photographs.

The Royal Naval Air Service (R.N.A.S.) received nearly two hundred Nieuport 10s and 12s and these were employed in the Aegean as well as on the Western Front. A number of these were subsequently transferred to the Royal Flying Corps (R.F.C.) to add to their existing stable of Nieuports. But with the appearance of the Nieuport 11 those remaining in service were gradually withdrawn to fulfil training duties.

Late in 1917 the American Expeditionary Forces (A.E.F.) purchased approximately 560 Nieuport 12s, and its variants, to be used for training purposes.

> ### *Nieuport Nie 12 Specifications*
>
> Performance
>
> | | |
> |---|---|
> | Wingspan: | 29 ft 8 ins (9.04 m) |
> | Length: | 24 ft 0 ins (7.31 m) |
> | Height: | 8 ft 9 ins (2.66 m) |
> | Weight empty: | 1,210 lbs (549 kg) |
> | Weight loaded: | 2,030 lbs (920 kg) |
> | Maximum speed: | 109 mph (175 km/h) |
> | Duration: | 3 hours |
> | Ceiling: | 15,400 ft (4,700 m) |
> | Armament: | One fixed forward-firing Lewis machine-gun Later aircraft added one synchronised .303 Vickers machine-gun. |
> | Engine: | 110-hp or 130-hp Clerget rotary. |

Nieuport Nie. 11 & 16

The French Nieuport Company was one of the most successful for the designs it produced during World War One, in particular the Type 11, and many of the French Aces considered it was second to none. With its sesqui lower wing it was

Nieuport 11

extremely manoeuvrable and was produced in large numbers, moreover its design was used for all Nieuport fighter types up, and including the Type 27.

When Gustave Delage joined the Nieuport company in January 1914 he immediately set to work on the design of a single-seater biplane with a 80-hp Gnôme rotary engine that would compete in the 1914 Gordon Bennett race. Due to the onset of World War I the race was cancelled but Delage's design was accepted by the *Aviation Militaire* and production got under way to fulfil the French government's requirement for fighter aircraft. It entered service in the summer of 1915 and quickly became a favourite with French and British pilots alike. Its outstanding manoeuvrability and rapid rate of climb together with its relatively diminutive size soon earned it the affectionate nickname of *Bébé* (Baby). Legendary pilots, such as Jean Navarre, Georges Guynemer, Charles Nungesser, Albert Ball and Billy Bishop were immediately attracted to this fabled aircraft and soon were amassing victories over the hitherto scourge of the German Fokker monoplanes.

In common with most Allied aircraft at that time it had a fixed Lewis machine-gun mounted above the upper wing and was angled to fire above the arc of the propeller.

The British R.N.A.S. and R.F.C. were quick to see the advantages of the Nieuport 11 and ordered a number that saw service on the Western Front. Orders for the aircraft were also received from Belgium, Italy and Russia. Italy not only bought direct from Nieuport but also obtained a licence to build them. In all Macchi built over 600 Nieuport 11s and these remained in service with the Italian and Albanian Air Services until mid 1917. The Netherlands also bought five and built a further twenty under licence.

The Nieuport 11 served with both No. 1 Wing and No. 3 Wing R.N.A.S. but while it was in service with the R.F.C. no accredited serial numbers were recorded. This has led to some confusion as five serial numbers were allocated to a 'Nieuport 13'. There was no type '13' and it is thought that they referred to Nieuport 11s and that '13' was a reference to their metric wing area. This was also a common practice with the Nieuport 17 where reference was made of a '15', again the wing area of the 17.

By the end of 1916 the Nieuport 11s abilities were being out-performed by the new designs of the Albatros and Fokker. Also it had suffered a number of losses through the weakness of the lower wing structure and was being systematically withdrawn from active service.

An experimental triplane was developed from the basic design of the Nieuport 11 but although a version of this was flown in early 1917 it did not receive the relevant backing to be put into production.

Nieuport Nie 11C.1 Specifications

Performance

Wingspan:	24 ft 9 ins (7.54 m)
Length:	19 ft 0 ins (5.80 m)
Height:	8 ft 0 ins (2.44 m)
Weight empty:	774 lbs (351 kg)
Weight loaded:	1,058 lbs (480 kg)
Maximum speed:	97 mph (156 km/h)
Duration:	2 ½ hours
Ceiling:	15,000 ft (4,580 m)
Armament:	One fixed forward-firing Lewis machine-gun.
Engine:	800-hp Le Rhône rotary.

Dudley Hill, a member of Escadrille Lafayette, sitting in Raoul Lufbery's Nieuport II

A more powerful variant made its appearance in 1916: this was the Nieuport 16 and was powered by a 110-hp Le Rhône engine and, instead of the fixed, over-wing Lewis machine-gun, it incorporated a synchronised Vickers machine-gun that the pilot could fire through the propeller without leaving his seat. Le

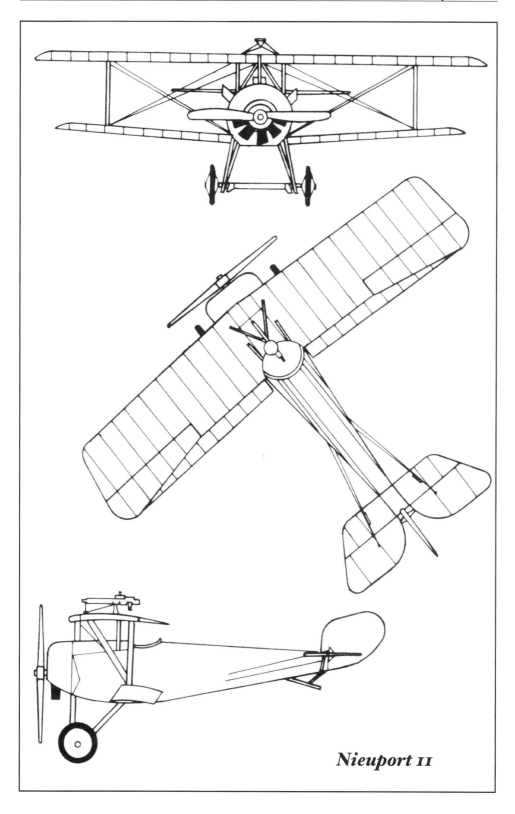

Nieuport 11

Prieur rockets were fitted to some Nieuport 16s. They were fitted on the interplane struts and achieved limited success in shooting down observation balloons. Although the R.N.A.S. had no recorded Nieuport 16s on their strength, they were certainly with No. 29 and No. 60 squadrons of the R.F.C. One of the last Nieuport 12s to be withdrawn from service was that used by Charles Guynemer and carried the famous '*Vieux Charles*' insignia.

Nieuport Nie. 17

Over the next two years the variations of the Nieuport fighter increased until the middle of 1916 when the Nieuport Nie 17 was produced.

Powered initially by a 110-hp Le Rhône engine the Nieuport N17 had a single spar lower wing and an enlarged wing area, 1474 sq. ft., as opposed to the Nieuport N11, which had a wing area of 1330 sq. ft. The early models had a cowling made of aluminium, which was in two halves but, due to problems, this was replaced with a horseshoe configuration. The construction of the fuselage consisted of metal tubing in the engine section, ash longerons in front of the

Nieuport 17 of No.. 6(N) Squadron. Lost on 6 June 1917 when it was shot down by Vzfw. Riesinger of Jasta 12.

cockpit and spruce longerons in the aft section behind the cockpit toward the tail. The fuselage behind the cockpit was covered in doped fabric until just before the tail where it was reinforced with plywood panels.

Ailerons were fitted to the top wing only and the tail surfaces were constructed of a light steel tubing and covered in fabric. The landing gear consisted of an aluminium cross member between the 'V' legs of the undercarriage and a steel tube axle, to which were fixed rubber shock absorbers.

Nieuport 17.

The aircraft was armed with a synchronised forward firing Vickers machine-gun fixed to the centreline of the forward fuselage. Ammunition was supplied via drums of canvas ammunition-belts stored within the fuselage fairings. Facilities to carry four Le Prieur anti-balloon rockets were mounted on each wing strut. Later models had the machine-gun mounted off-centre and some even had twin, unsynchronised, Lewis machine-guns mounted on the upper wing. The Nieuport N17 had a variety of roles including that of a high-speed photo-reconnaissance aircraft with a 26-cm camera mounted behind the pilot's seat.

A number of engines were tried out in the Nieuport 17, a 130-hp Clerget 9b, a 9z and a 120-hp Le Rhône. The latter engine was used in the Nieuport 17 *bis*, the only variation of the 17 and, of which, only a small number were produced. However, one of these variations became the favourite aircraft of the French ace Charles Nungesser, who used it to great effect. The 17 also saw limited

Nieuport 17 belonging to the Finnish Air Force.

service with the Royal Naval Air Service but although, initially, the aircraft was welcomed by the French fighter pilots, they soon realised that it was outclassed by the contemporary German fighters. The pilots demands for a better aircraft prompted some attempts to improve the Nieuport 17, but without great success.

There were a number of problems discovered by both R.F.C. and Italian pilots when the aircraft was flown under battle conditions. During certain manoeuvres the aircraft's lower wing spar had a tendency to break and it was with a certain trepidation that the aircraft was flown.

Two hundred and seventy-four Nieuport 17s were supplied to the Royal Flying Corps, while a small number of Nieuport 17 *Escadrilles* were assigned to serve with the *Groupes de Combat* that supported the *armées*. A number of other countries purchased the aircraft, Belgium, Chile, Colombia, Czechoslovakia, Estonia, Hungary, Finland, Netherlands, Italy, Poland, Romania, Russia, Siam and the Ukraine.. Although in some peoples eyes the Nieuport 17 was not a great success, the fact that so many countries purchased it, albeit not in large numbers, showed that there was a great deal of confidence in the aircraft.

Nieuport Nie 17 Specifications

Performance

Wingspan:	26 ft 9 ins (8.16 m)
Length:	19 ft 0 ins (5.80 m)
Height:	7 ft 10 ins (2.40 m)
Weight empty:	827 lbs (375 kg)
Weight loaded:	1,235 lbs (560 kg)
Maximum speed:	109 mph (175 km/h)
Duration:	2 hours
Ceiling:	17,390 ft (5,300 m)
Armament:	One synchronised .303 Vickers machine-gun or two Lewis machine guns mounted on the upper wing. Some had 8 Le Prieur rockets fitted.
Engine:	110-hp Le Rhône 9Ja rotary.

Some of the countries that purchased the Nieuport 17, also built it under licence. The Russian version, with a 110-hp Le Rhône 9Ja engine, was built by the Dux and Mosca firms in Russia. The Italian version, with a 120-hp Le Rhône engine, was built by Macchi, who produced a total of 150 aircraft.

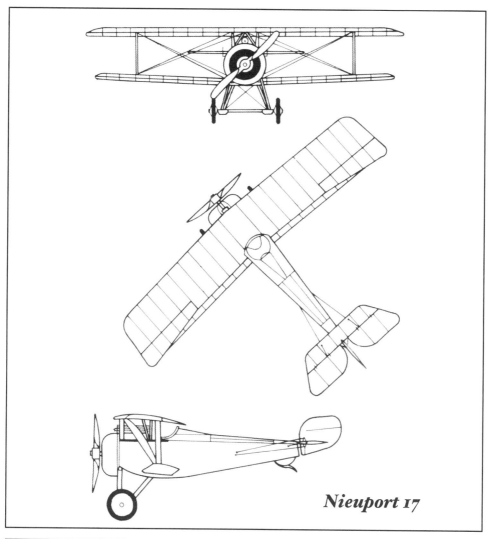

Nieuport 17

Nieuport 17. Note the experimental triangular windscreen.

Nieuport 17 belonging to the Imperial Russian Air Service at Kiev in 1917.

A Nieuport 17 of Escadrille *Lafayette, July 1917.*

A Nieuport 17 fitted with a 130-hp Clerget engine and large spinner.

A Nieuport 17 fitted with a 130-hp Clerget engine and large spinner.

Originally a Nieuport 17 converted to a Type 23 with a lengthened and rounded fuselage.

Nieuport 20 two-seater No. .A6602 at Harlaxton, Nr. Grantham, Lincolnshire in 1917.

Nieuport Nie 21

The required improvements in the design of the Nieuport 17 brought about the development of the Nieuport Nie 21.

This aircraft incorporated the best features of the Nieuport 11 and the 17. It had a lightened fuselage, which was based on that of the 11 and had the wings of the 17 – although the parallel and bracing wires were altered somewhat. Surprisingly, although the Nieuport 17 had been powered by a 110-hp Le Rhône engine, the finished Nieuport 21 had a reduced 80-hp Le Rhône 9C.

It was originally designed as a fighter-trainer, although there were thoughts about the possibilities of using it as a high-altitude bomber escort. Less than 100 were built, a number of which went to the Imperial Russian Air Service,

Nieuport Nie 21 Specifications

Performance

Wingspan:	26 ft 9 ins (8.16 m)
Length:	19 ft 0 ins (5.80 m)
Height:	7 ft 10 ins (2.40 m)
Weight empty:	770 lbs (350 kg)
Weight loaded:	1,170 lbs (530 kg)
Maximum speed:	94 mph (150 km/h)
Duration:	2 hours Ceiling: 17,000 ft (5,200 m)
Armament:	One synchronised .303 Vickers machine-gun
Engine:	80-hp Le Rhône 9C rotary.

Sgt Ted Ditchburn of 40 Squadron, R.F.C., checking the engine on his Nieuport 23 at Treizennes airfield - March 1917.

leaving the higher-powered Nieuport 17 for the French *Escadrilles*. At least four of these aircraft were supplied to the French Navy in 1920 for launch training purposes from the *Bapaume*.

Only four other countries, besides Russia, purchased the Nieuport 21 – Brazil, Great Britain, Ukraine and the United States. The Russian manufacturer Dux built 68 of the aircraft under licence.

Nieuport 23s of No. 40 Squadron at Treizennes preparing to take off on patrol.

Capitain Geroges Guynemer in his Nieuport 23 - 1916.

Raoul Lufbery of the Lafayette Escadrille *in the cockpit of his Nieuport 27. To the left is Captain Soubiran and Lieutenant Didier Soubiran.*

Nieuport Nie 23

The appearance of the Nieuport 23 was one of those developments that, on the face of it, heralded a new type of aircraft. But it differed from the Nieuport 17 in only a few minor details, the main one being that it was fitted with a new type of interrupter gear. This required the .303 Vickers machine-gun to be fitted slightly to starboard of the centreline. The remaining changes were so minor that it was almost impossible to tell the difference between the two aircraft.

The aircraft was powered by two types of engine, the 110-hp Le Rhône 9Ja and the 120-hp Le Rhône 9Jb. Some of the early models were fitted with the 80-hp Le Rhône engine and used as trainers. As with earlier models the Nieuport 23 was built under licence by the Dax factory in Russia and was powered by the 120-hp Le Rhône 9Jb engine.

As with its predecessor, the Nieuport 21, there were problems with the lower wings. This manifested itself during combat and accidents occurred when the aircraft was subjected to violent manoeuvres. On a number of occasions sections of the lower wings were seen to break off, causing the death of Allied pilots. The French *General Chef de Service* issued an order stating that the Nieuport 23 would be allowed to fly only if the following modifications were made immediately:

Additional cables to be fitted to reinforce the wings. The lower wings of the Type 23 to be replaced with the Type 24 wings.

Nieuport 27 powered by a 130-hp Le Rhône rotary engine.

One hundred and fifty sets of wings were requested as replacements and nine countries, Belgium (4); Czechoslovakia (5); Finland (2 Dux built); Poland (3); Russia (1 – the remainder having been built under licence); Switzerland (5); Ukraine (7); Great Britain (30) and the USA (50), were also informed of the problem and modifications were made.

Nieuport Nie. 28C.1

New and better German and British designs soon outpaced the nimble Nieuport and work was started in early 1917 to produce a replacement. This took the form of the Model 28, of which a prototype, serial 4434, flew for the first time on June 14, 1917. It was a completely new design as the 'normal' Nieuport wing system was dropped and a set of almost equal span wings were adopted.

It was an excellent design and quickly adopted by the French and put into mass production as the Model 28C-I. However, like the Hurricane and Spitfire designs of World War Two the Nieuport 28 had a rival fighter, the superb SPAD which had a maximum speed of 138mph to the 28's 122.

As a result the French Air Force preferred the SPAD XIII and this fighter replaced the Nieuport as their front line aeroplane. There was an immediate problem as the Nieuport factory was geared up, and producing, the Model 28 and these events could not easily be halted.

Nieuport 17s at Aviation Field No.4, Issoudon on 21 May 1918.

The solution was eventually resolved when America entered the war on the Allied side. As a nation never involved before in an European war it was severely handicapped by having an Air Force that was virtually without equipment. Purchasing missions were sent to Britain and France to evaluate possible equipment, in particular aircraft, and placed orders for two fighters, the British S.E.5A and SPAD XIII.

Although America had decided that it would not purchase foreign war material direct from the supplier, preferring to build it under licence and so keep its factories busy, there was not the time to arrange this situation. An acceptable solution was to order the two fighters direct from the manufacturers and supply all the Allied Air Forces from the European companies.

There was a second problem, despite the large American orders French and British aircraft companies did not possess the manufacturing equivalent of the Americans, and the almost impossible problem was resolved when the A.E.F. agreed to equip its fighter squadrons with a mix of the Nieuport and SPAD, with the former being supplied in the greater quantity.

Why did the French Air Force, and Americans, prefer the SPAD. Apart from the little difference in speed they were both designs of equal quality. Indeed,

Nieuport 17s at Aviation Field No.. 4, Issoudon on 21 May 1918.

contemporary technical reports of the period stated 'that the Nieuport 28 was an excellent fighter'. But, those same sources said of the SPAD, `It is in the front rank for speed and climb and is recognised as the finest *aeroplane de Chasse, destroyer.*

Model 28's Genesis

Although the Nieuport line of fighters were of their time, the pace of air battles had increased and the basic design was not strong enough to absorb the huge stresses upon the rather flimsy airframes of the Models 11,16 and 17. The basic 'V'-strut sesqui-plane design had reached its limit with the Model 24, and before this, and the follow-on Model 27 had entered service, Nieuport was experimenting with a completely new design.

Out would go the well-known and tried sesqui-plane and in came the strengthened airframe and equi-span wing of parallel chord. This was installed on an experimental model of the 24 together with a new Gnome rotary engine of 160-hp.

Trials proved the new items and it was decided to design, and build a prototype. It had a wire braced wooden fuselage built up around four longerons that was fabric covered. It was four feet longer than that of the Model 24. The longitudinal stringers were supported by rounded formers to provide and elegant configuration that was a departure from previous, slab sided models.

The wings had wooden frames, spars and ribs, as did the tail unit, and although the wing was fabric covered, the tail surfaces were covered with a thin gauge fibreboard and were similar to those of the Model 24/27. The stronger undercarriage was built up from aluminium tubes for strength/weight considerations. The engine was enclosed in a deep cowling that had been

Nieuport Nie 28C.1 Specifications

Wingspan: 26 ft 9 ins (8.16 m)
Length: 21 ft 0 ins (640 m)
Height: 8 ft 2 ins (2.50 m)
Weight empty: 1005 lbs (456 kg)
Weight loaded: 1,540 lbs (698 kg)
Maximum speed: 123 mph (198 km/h)
Duration: $1^1/_2$ hours
Ceiling: 17,000 ft (5,200 m)
Armament: two synchronised .303 Vickers
          machine-guns
Engine: 160-hp Gnôme Monosoupape
          9Nc rotary.

Nieuport 28

A captured Nieuport 28 in German markings.

developed for the Model 24 experimental prototype. The wings had single interplane struts and were not supported by wires.

There were problems right from the start when it was discovered that if the aircraft was put into a steep dive the fabric on the wings started to shred. The original engine also added to the problems, it was the new, nine-cylinder Gnôme 9-N rotary, air cooled unit of 160/170-hp which had a tendency to catch fire. Some of the early aircraft also had the Le Rhône motor which could be controlled by the throttle from 1250 to 900 rpm. Later production models had the Gnôme 10-hp unit 'Monosoupapes' engine fitted. Armament was sparse, being a single Vickers .303in machine-gun outboard of the port, centre section struts. It was soon increased to two, with the second situated on the fuselage in front of the pilot. A number of A.E.F. Model 28s had the American Marlin gun of 0.30 inch, and a few had a single 11 mm. Vickers. Nieuport 28C-Is equipped the 27th, 94th and 147th Aero Squadrons in France, first deliveries being in

A US Navy Nieuport 28.

March 1918.

The production life of the Model 28 was short as it could not attain the same performance of the SPAD. As a result production was run-down as the Nieuport factory installed a new line for the production of its rival, the SPAD. A total of 297 were delivered to the A.E.F. until sufficient quantities of the SPAD were available as from July 1918 and the Nieuports relegated to the training role.

Captain Kenneth Marr leaning on his Nieuport 28 with the 'Hat-in-the-Ring' insignia of the US 94th Aero Squadron, May 1918.

A decorated Nieuport 17 of the 3rd Aerial Instruction Centre in France, May 1918.

The aircraft was rejected by the *Aviation Militaire*, but was accepted by America as, at that time, they were in desperate need of fighter aircraft. The Model 28 was not missed due to its tendencies to shed its upper wing fabric and part of the leading edge ribs, and the unreliable Gnome Monosoupape engine. Numerous engines were installed and tested such as the Clerget, Hispano-Suiza and Lorraines. Fifty were shipped back to America in 1919 with twelve being transferred to the Navy for use on its battleships where they were flown from a platform built over the front gun turret. A small number of this batch were fitted with hydrovanes ahead of the undercarriage to keep them from nosing over if they ditched by keeping the nose up until the floatation gear inflated. All were sold, or scrapped and as far as is known three still exist. A small batch was sold to the Royal Hellenic Army Air Service.

Combat at last

It was the American Expeditionary Forces (A.E.F.). that was to use the Model 28C-I for battle, and to any effect, when the four squadrons of the First Pursuit Group ordered the 95th to patrol the front line on March 15, 1918. This was well before the final battles of the war started when General Haig's British Army launched it attack through Flanders supported by hundreds of the new British tanks and Sopwith Camels of the R.A.F's fighter squadrons.

The first contact with the enemy was on April 14, 1918, when a flight of three American aircraft from the 94th Squadron, led by Lieutenant Eddie

Rickenbacker., were returning to their base. They intercepted two German fighters that appeared over the airfield and were able to chase them away. The first real victory, however, was a Pfalz D.III which was shot down in flames and an Albatros D.V forced to land. The next victory was on May 2 when an Albatros D.V was shot down, but during the encounter the Nieuports old problem of stripping the fabric from the top wing when in a dive, reappeared. Fortunately the American pilot managed to keep control of his aircraft and return safely.

Lieutenant Andrew Campbell standing in the gap where his portside left lower wing used to be on his Nieuport 17.

Colour schemes

The prototype and a number of production Type 28s were finished in the normal Nieuport silver-grey scheme. When used in combat the standard French schemes of upper and fuselage side surfaces were painted in a pattern of Dark Green and olive and sand. The wing and fuselage surfaces were clear doped as was the tailplane. Most aircraft carried the French standard roundel of Red (outer), White and Blue (centre) on the underside and upper of the wings and also the underside of the lower wing.

Early deliveries to the American Expeditionary Forces carried the American White centres under the upper wing but this was to be discontinued. Neither the French or American used roundels on the fuselage. The early Type 28s had rudder stripes to fin and rudder (Red, White and Blue) with the French and R.F.C. having the Red on the trailing edge.

When the Americans used their new circular marking to replace the White star of 1917 they used the old Russian marks of a Red centre, then White and finally the Blue outer ring. The French painted the American aircraft's fin/rudder in stripes of Red, White and Blue but the Americans used a Blue front, followed by White and a Red centre. Individual American aircraft in the squadrons had large block numbers on each side of the fuselage in White, outlined Black and Black. The 27th Squadron had an American 'Hat-in-the-Ring' insignia and the 94th, a kicking Army Mule. A Scotch terrier marking was used by the 147th Pursuit Squadron but it was unauthorised.

In 1919, when the American fighter units took their Nieuport N.28s back to the States, they were normally over painted in standard U.S. Army Olive Drab with white stars replacing the wing roundels. Navy N.28s were painted a Light Grey overall and also had the white Star insignia.

Charles Nunggesser with his Nieuport 17, N1895, converted to a Type 24-bis which incorporated a streamlined fuselage and a 130-hp British Bentley rotary A.R.1 engine.

Another view of Nungesser's Nieuport 17 showing his personal 'Death's Head' insignia.

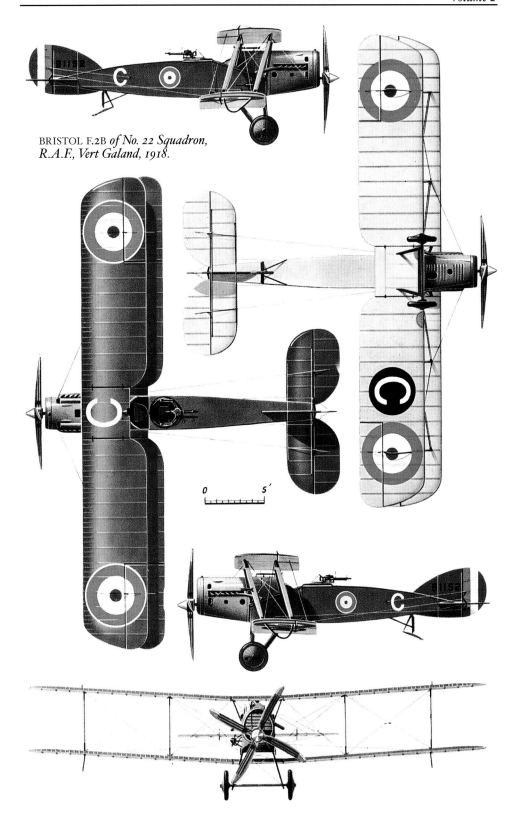

BRISTOL F.2B *of No. 22 Squadron,*
R.A.F., Vert Galand, 1918.

0   5'

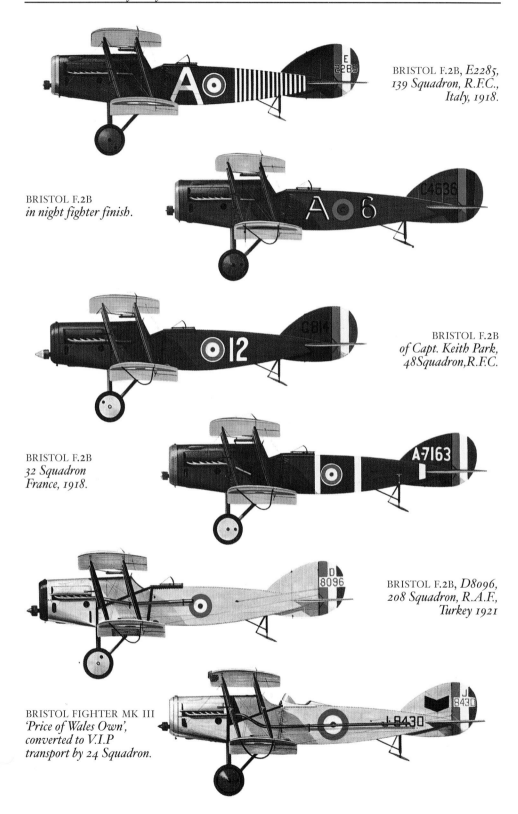

BRISTOL F.2B, *E2285,*
139 Squadron, R.F.C.,
Italy, 1918.

BRISTOL F.2B
in night fighter finish.

BRISTOL F.2B
of Capt. Keith Park,
48Squadron,R.F.C.

BRISTOL F.2B
32 Squadron
France, 1918.

BRISTOL F.2B, *D8096,*
208 Squadron, R.A.F.,
Turkey 1921

BRISTOL FIGHTER MK III
'Price of Wales Own',
converted to V.I.P
transport by 24 Squadron.

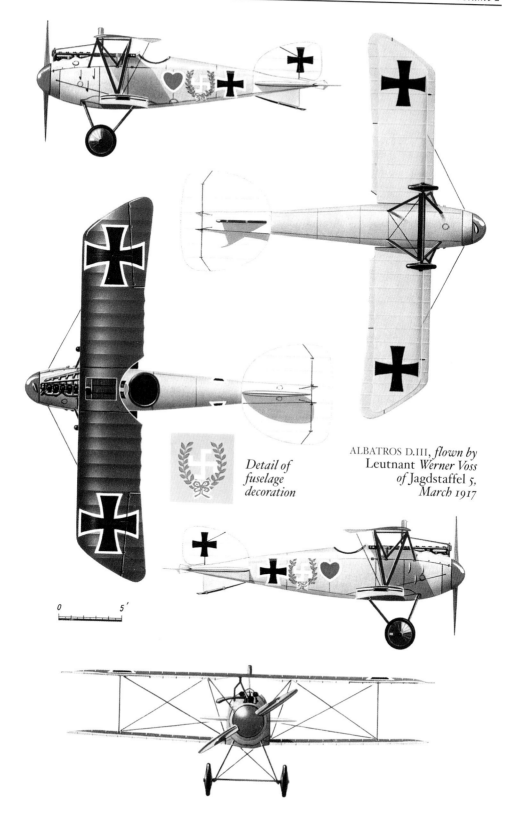

*Detail of
fuselage
decoration*

ALBATROS D.III, *flown by*
Leutnant *Werner Voss
of* Jagdstaffel 5,
March 1917

0   5′

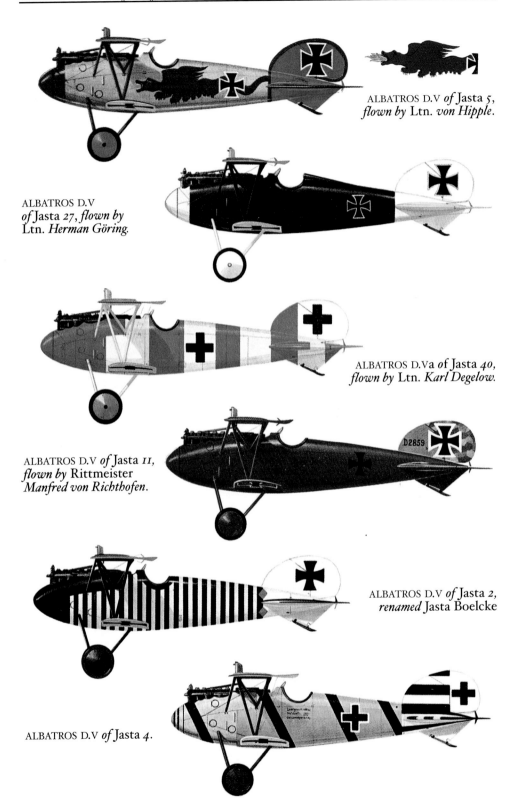

ALBATROS D.V *of* Jasta 5,
flown by Ltn. *von Hipple.*

ALBATROS D.V
of Jasta 27, *flown by*
Ltn. *Herman Göring.*

ALBATROS D.Va *of* Jasta 40,
flown by Ltn. *Karl Degelow.*

ALBATROS D.V *of* Jasta 11,
flown by Rittmeister
Manfred von Richthofen.

ALBATROS D.V *of* Jasta 2,
renamed Jasta Boelcke

ALBATROS D.V *of* Jasta 4.

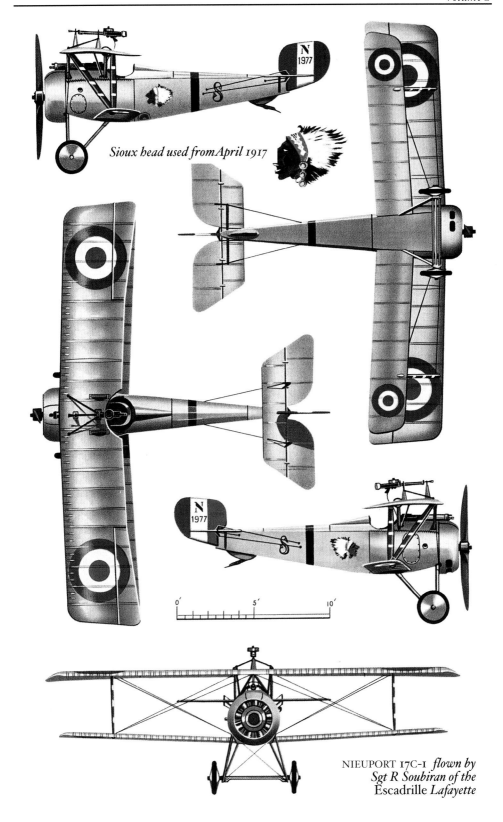

Sioux head used from April 1917

NIEUPORT 17C-1 *flown by*
Sgt R Soubiran of the
Escadrille *Lafayette*

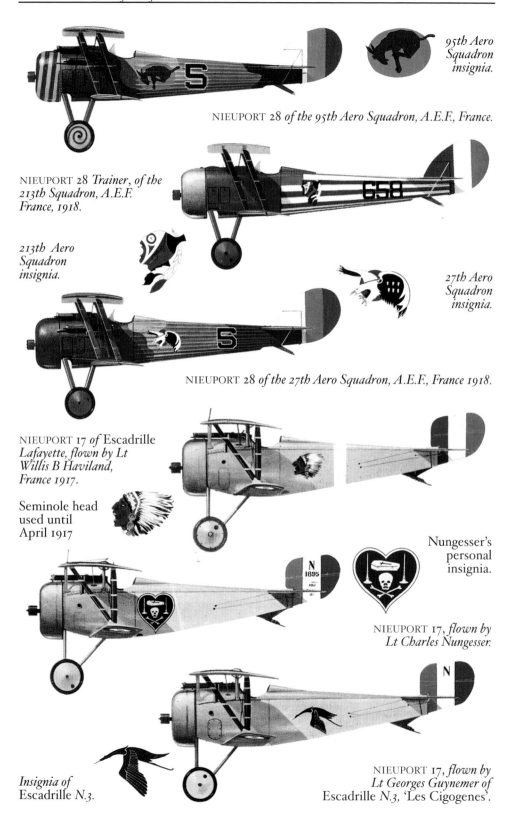

95th Aero
Squadron
insignia.

NIEUPORT 28 *of the 95th Aero Squadron, A.E.F., France.*

NIEUPORT 28 *Trainer, of the
213th Squadron, A.E.F.
France, 1918.*

*213th Aero
Squadron
insignia.*

27th Aero
Squadron
insignia.

NIEUPORT 28 *of the 27th Aero Squadron, A.E.F., France 1918.*

NIEUPORT 17 *of* Escadrille
*Lafayette, flown by Lt
Willis B Haviland,
France 1917.*

Seminole head
used until
April 1917

Nungesser's
personal
insignia.

NIEUPORT 17, *flown by
Lt Charles Nungesser.*

*Insignia of
Escadrille N.3.*

NIEUPORT 17, *flown by
Lt Georges Guynemer of
Escadrille N.3, 'Les Cigogenes'.*

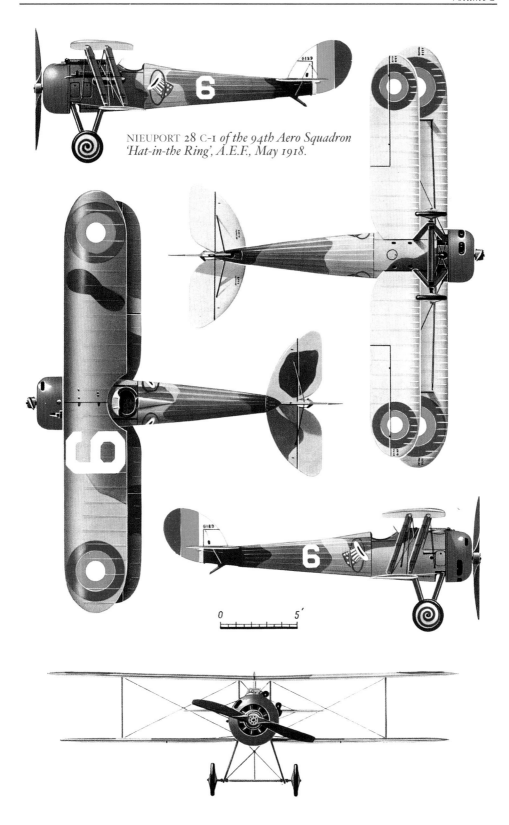

NIEUPORT 28 C-1 *of the 94th Aero Squadron*
'Hat-in-the Ring', A.E.F., May 1918.

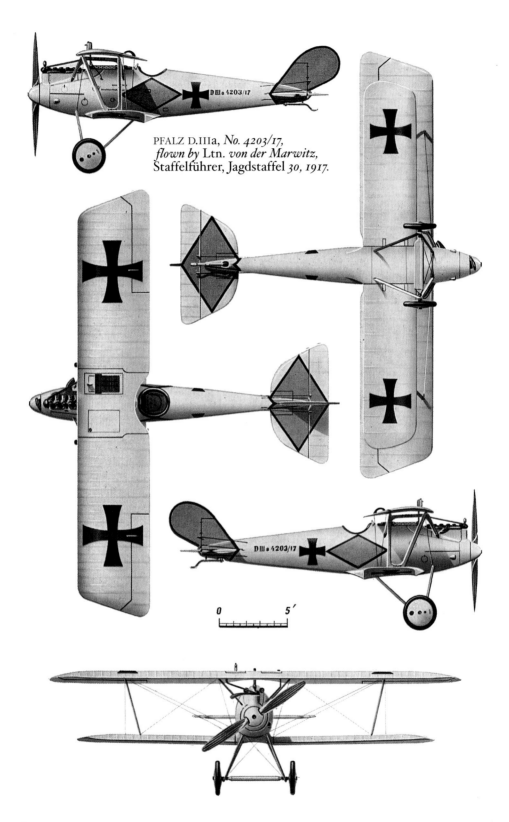

PFALZ D.IIIa, *No. 4203/17,*
flown by Ltn. *von der Marwitz,*
Staffelführer, Jagdstaffel *30, 1917.*

0   5´

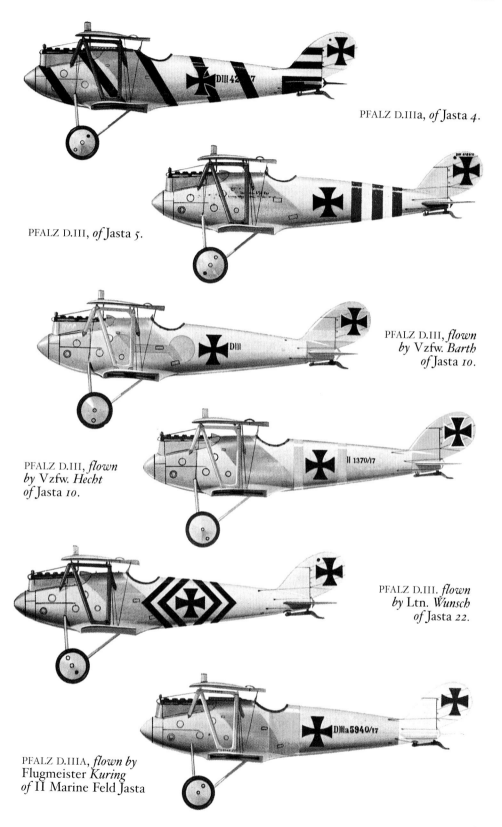

PFALZ D.IIIa, *of* Jasta 4.

PFALZ D.III, *of* Jasta 5.

PFALZ D.III, *flown by* Vzfw. *Barth of* Jasta 10.

PFALZ D.III, *flown by* Vzfw. *Hecht of* Jasta 10.

PFALZ D.III. *flown by* Ltn. *Wunsch of* Jasta 22.

PFALZ D.IIIA, *flown by* Flugmeister *Kuring of* II Marine Feld Jasta

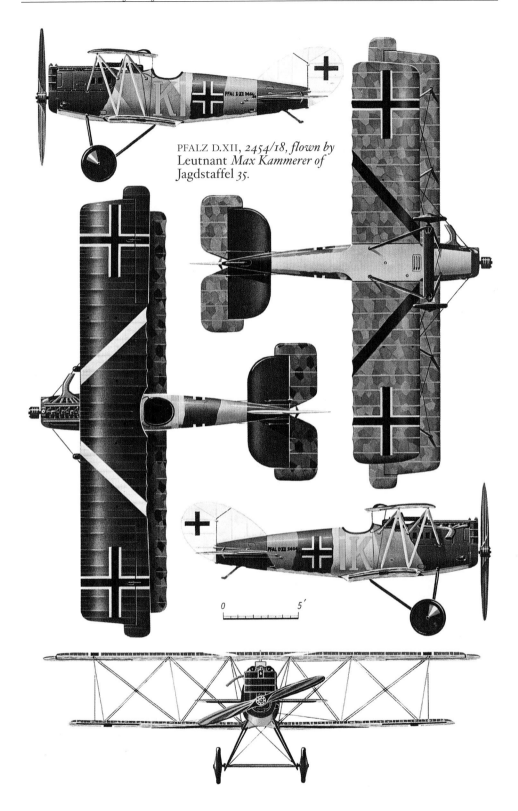

PFALZ D.XII, *2454/18, flown by* Leutnant *Max Kammerer of* Jagdstaffel *35.*

0   5′

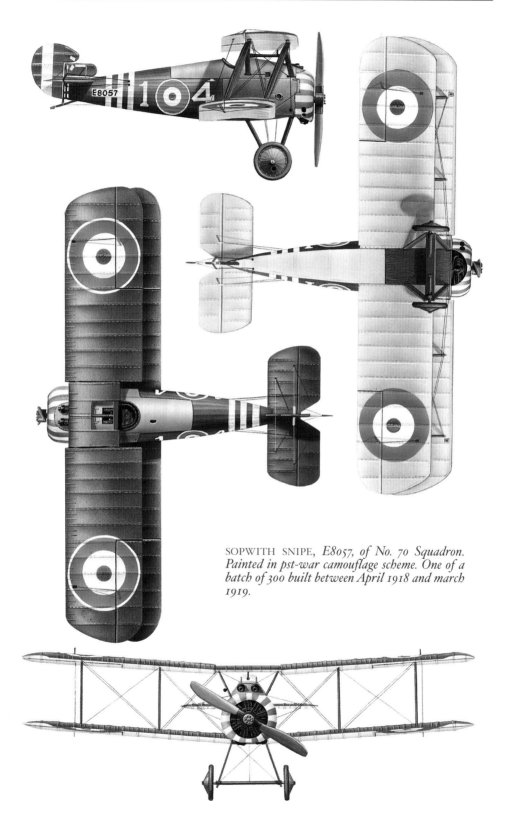

SOPWITH SNIPE, *E8057, of No. 70 Squadron.*
Painted in pst-war camouflage scheme. One of a
batch of 300 built between April 1918 and march
1919.

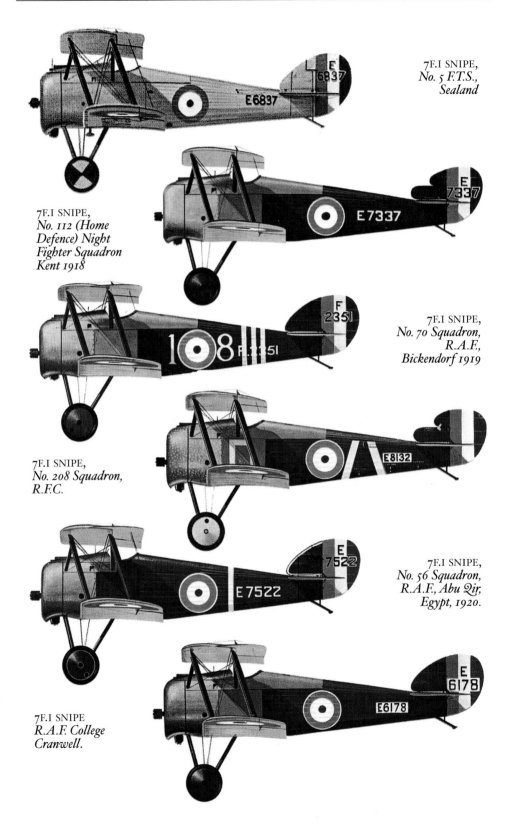

7F.I SNIPE,
No. 5 F.T.S.,
Sealand

7F.I SNIPE,
No. 112 (Home
Defence) Night
Fighter Squadron
Kent 1918

7F.I SNIPE,
No. 70 Squadron,
R.A.F.,
Bickendorf 1919

7F.I SNIPE,
No. 208 Squadron,
R.F.C.

7F.I SNIPE,
No. 56 Squadron,
R.A.F., Abu Qir,
Egypt, 1920.

7F.I SNIPE
R.A.F. College
Cranwell.

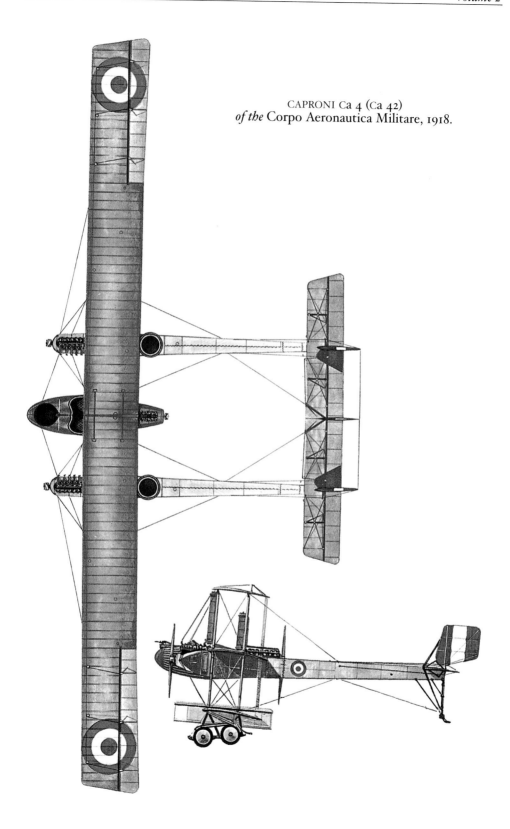

CAPRONI Ca 4 (Ca 42)
of the Corpo Aeronautica Militare, 1918.

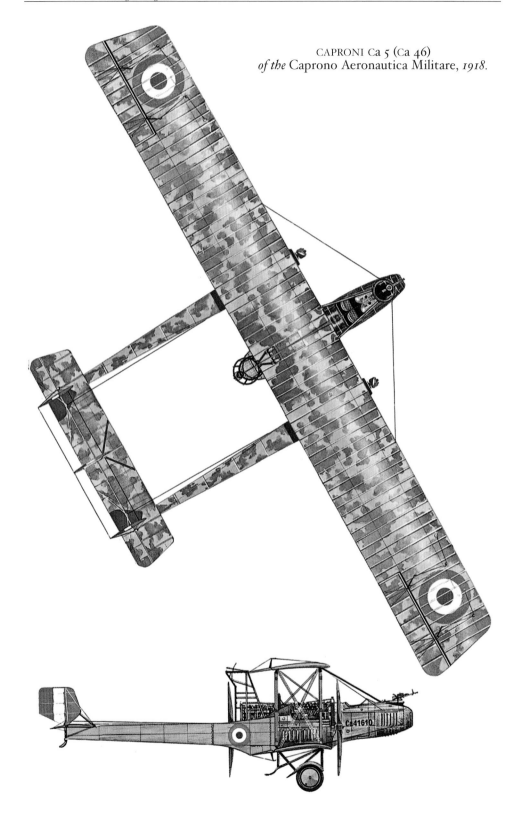

CAPRONI Ca 5 (Ca 46)
of the Caprono Aeronautica Militare, *1918.*

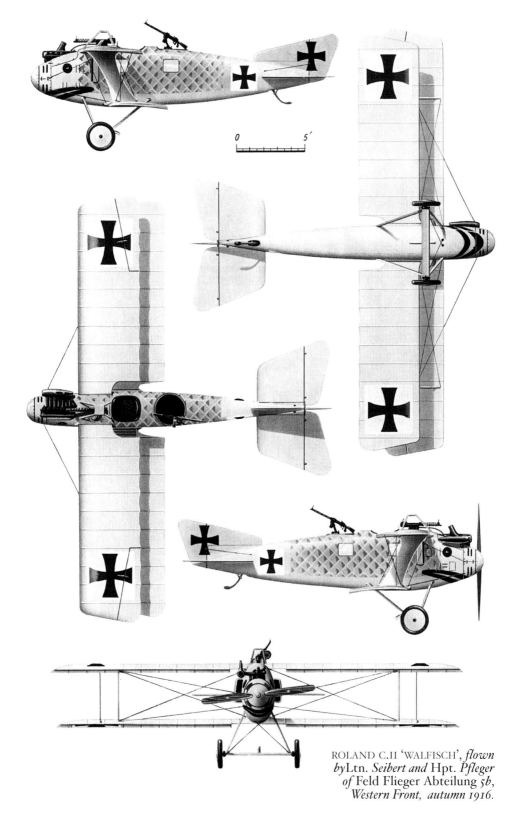

ROLAND C.II 'WALFISCH', *flown by*Ltn. *Seibert and* Hpt. *Pfleger of* Feld Flieger Abteilung *5b, Western Front, autumn 1916.*

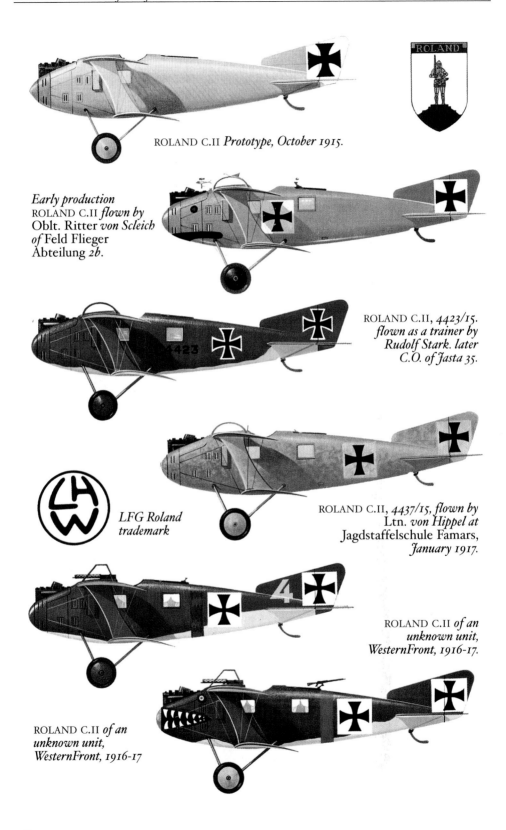

ROLAND C.II *Prototype, October 1915.*

Early production ROLAND C.II *flown by* Oblt. Ritter *von Scleich* of Feld Flieger Abteilung *2b.*

ROLAND C.II, *4423/15.* *flown as a trainer by* *Rudolf Stark. later* *C.O. of Jasta 35.*

LFG Roland trademark

ROLAND C.II, *4437/15, flown by* Ltn. *von Hippel at* Jagdstaffelschule Famars, *January 1917.*

ROLAND C.II *of an* *unknown unit,* WesternFront, *1916-17.*

ROLAND C.II *of an* *unknown unit,* WesternFront, *1916-17*

CHAPTER FOUR

Pfalz Fighters

Germany, prior to the First World War, was a country made up of a number of minor Kingdoms and Principalities. Among them was the Kingdom of Bavaria which, after Prussia, was the second most powerful state in the German Second Reich. Bavaria enjoyed considerable autonomy and military privileges, and at the onset of the First World War had its own air service, War Ministry and General Staff. There was an underlying bitter rivalry between some of the states as became apparent when bravery awards were given. There were even *Jastas* made up of only Bavarians or Prussians in the early stages of the war. Unlike the other states, Bavaria's armed forces were only under the command of the Emperor *Kaiser* Wilhelm in time of war.

With the threat of the First World War looming, three brothers, Alfred, Walter and Ernst Eversbusch established an aircraft manufacturing plant with the financial aid of the Bavarian Government. The government were concerned that unless they contributed to the manufacture of the aircraft they would have

L-R: Oberleutnant *Seibert,* Leutnant *Klein, Alfred Eversbusch,* Leutnant *Ernt Udet,* Leutnant *Kreft,* KuK Oberleutnant *Lucas* and Dr *Moericke. This photograph was taken whilst the pilots were on a visit to the Pfalz factory.*

no say in the equipment that would be used by the Bavarian pilots. Initially the intention was to approach the Albatros company and to acquire the rights to build their aircraft in Bavaria, but negotiations fell through. Then the Bavarian Flying Service stepped in and at their instigation the Pfalz company approached Gustav Otto, a financier who helped finance the new company and assisted in the development of the business. They also acquired the rights to build the *Otto* biplane. The *Pfalz Flugzeug-Werke* was built at Speyer am Rhein in July 1913. The first aircraft to be produced there was not one of their own designs, but the Otto pusher biplane which was powered by a 100-hp Rapp engine.

Later Alfred Eversbusch managed to obtain a licence from the French Morane-Saulnier company to manufacture the 'L' type Parasol monoplane. The first Parasol was built at the end of 1914 but only a few of these were built. It is interesting to note that the cockpit had transparent sides which upon reflection was totally unnecessary because the downward view was excellent without them.

The Pfalz A.II.

The next model was later given a military designation of the Pfalz A.I and powered with a 80-hp seven-cylinder, Oberursel U.o rotary engine. Their role was for photo-reconnaissance and scouting missions. There was a Pfalz A.II, which was no more than an A.I with a 100-hp nine-cylinder Oberursel U.I rotary engine fitted.

Pfalz A.I & A.II Specifications

Performance

Wingspan:	36 ft 7 ins. (11.2 m).
Length:	22 ft 6 ins. (6.9 m).
Height:	11 ft 2 ins. (3.4 m).
Weight Empty:	804 lb. (365 kg.).
Weight Loaded:	1,309 lb. (595 kg.).
Maximum speed:	84 mph.
Duration:	4 hours - A.I, 2 hours - A.II.
Armament:	None
Engine:	80-hp Oberursel U.o. (A.I)
	100-hp Oberursel U.I (A.II)

Pfalz 'E' Series

At the same time as acquiring a licence to build the Morane-Saulnier 'L' type, Pfalz also obtained permission to build the 'H' type, which was re-designated the Pfalz E.I and fitted with the 80-hp Oberursel U.o seven-cylinder engine. Walter Eversbusch, the youngest of the three brothers, enrolled in the Morane-Saulnier flying school near Paris in the spring of 1914 from where he graduated with his flying licence. He became the company's test pilot but was killed on June 1, 1916 when he crashed testing one of the company's aircraft.

The Pfalz E.I on its tail stand.

When the war began in August 1914, the company had produced only three Otto biplane pushers, which were immediately dispatched to the Bavarian squadrons. It soon became obvious that the Otto was seriously under-powered taking 15 minutes to reach a height of 2,500 ft and, considering they only had an operating ceiling of 3,600 ft, were not really that suitable for reconnaissance missions. There was also another problem, the Otto bore a strong resemblance to the French pusher aircraft and was often shot at by German infantrymen. It has to be remembered that German soldiers, and Allied soldiers, had rarely, if ever, seen an aircraft, let alone recognised it as one of their own. By December, fortunately for the pilots of these aircraft, the Otto had been replaced by Albatros B and L.V.G. models.

Pfalz E.I fresh from the factory showing the extensive identification markings on the aircraft.

As the war progressed large numbers of the Pfalz E.I were built but very few saw service on the Front line as they were assigned to Bavarian flying schools as unarmed trainers. A small number of the E.I. saw action in Macedonia, Syria and Palestine.

The Pfalz parasol was in action in Italy before the war between Germany and Italy had actually started. On July 31, 1915 a German aircraft, with simulated Austro-Hungarian markings covering the German crosses and flown by *Leutnant* Otto Kissenberth of *Feldflieger-Abteilung 9b*, attacked Italian Alpine positions. He dropped five 10kg Carbonit bombs on the positions causing a number of casualties. Fortunately the aircraft had a good rate of climb, for because of the high altitude position of the Italian troops, they were able to subject the aircraft to a heavy rate of fire. Otto Kissenberth managed to climb his Pfalz parasol aircraft away and out of danger.

Pfalz E.I Specifications

Performance

Wingspan:30 ft. 6_ ins. (9.2 m).
Length:20 ft. 6 ins. (6.3 m).
Height:11 ft. 1_ ins. (3.4 m).
Weight Empty: 760 lb. (345 kg.).
Weight Loaded: 1,179 lb. (535 kg.).
Maximum speed: 93.2 mph.
Duration: 1_ hour.
Armament: None. The last 50 were fitted with a single synchronised forward-firing Spandau machine-gun
Engine: 80-hp Oberursel U.o.

Pfalz E.I. about to take off on a test flight.

The first ten Pfalz E.Is were unarmed scouts, but with the development of synchronisation gearing, the remaining fifty were fitted with a fixed, forward-firing Spandau machine gun. In total sixty of these aircraft were built and sent to the Front. The Pfalz E.II was produced some months later, but this was just an E.I with the 100-hp Oberursel U.I nine-cylinder rotary engine fitted and with the synchronised Spandau machine gun. The E.II had a wingspan of 33 ft 4 in., which was slightly longer than that of the E.I. Such was the need for aircraft at this time, that the E.II was already in service with a number of the Bavarian squadrons, before the Idflieg *(Inspektion der Fliegentruppen)* had finished the *Typen-Prufung* (Acceptance Test), which wasn't completed until July 1916.

Pfalz E.II Specifications

Performance

Wingspan:	33 ft 4 ins. (10.2 m).
Length:	21 ft 2 ins. (6.45 m).
Height:	8 ft 3 ins. (2.55 m).
Weight Empty:	904 lb. (410 kg.).
Weight Loaded:	1,261 lb. (572 kg.).
Maximum speed:	93 mph.
Duration:	1 1/2 hours.
Armament:	One synchronised forward-firing Spandau machine-gun.
Engine:	100-hp Oberursel U.I.

Pfalz E.II.

Pfalz E.II with Unteroffizier *Max Holtzem at the controls about to take off.*

This was followed by the debut of the Pfalz E.III, which was in fact an armed version of the A.II parasol monoplane. Only six were built, four of which managed to make the Front line and see service. It was powered by a 100-hp Oberursel U.I rotary engine, had a wingspan of 36 ft 7 in. and a fuselage length of 22 ft 4 in.

Pfalz E.III being serviced by the ground crew.

Pfalz E.III Specifications

Performance

Wingspan:	36 ft 7 ins. (11.2 m).
Length:	22 ft 4 ins. (6.85 m).
Height:	11 ft 2 ins. (3.4 m).
Weight Empty:	981 lb. (445 kg.).
Weight Loaded:	1,554 lb. (705 kg.).
Maximum speed:	93 mph.
Duration:	2 hours.
Armament:	None.
Engine:	100-hp Oberursel U.I.

The next in the 'E' series of fighters, was the Pfalz E.IV. Almost identical to the other E-series fighters, the E.IV was fitted with the 160-hp two-row Oberursel U.III rotary engine. It had a wingspan of 33 ft 5 in., a fuselage length of 21 ft 6 in. a top speed of 100 mph and a climb rate of 1,300 feet per minute. It carried twin synchronised forward firing Spandau machine guns. This feisty little fighter was built, surprisingly, in small numbers, no more than twenty-five were known to have been manufactured.

Pfalz E.IV Specifications

Performance

Wingspan:	33 ft 5 ins. (10.2 m).
Length:	21 ft 6 ins. (6.6 m).
Height:	8 ft 2 ins. (2.55 m).
Weight Empty:	1,038 lb. (471 kg.).
Weight Loaded:	1,554 lb. (705 kg.).
Maximum speed:	100 mph.
Duration:	1 hour.
Armament:	Two synchronised forward-firing Spandau machine-guns.
Engine:	160-hp Oberursel U.III.

The last of the E-series fighters was the Pfalz E.V. Constructed on the standard E-type airframe, the E.V was powered by a 100-hp Mercedes D.I engine, giving the aircraft a top speed of 103 mph. This was a deviation from the rotary engines that powered the previous E-series of aircraft. It was armed with a synchronised forward firing Spandau machine gun and was only slightly different from the other Pfalz monoplanes by means of an enlarged and different shaped rudder.

Pfalz 'D' Series

The monoplane fighter was rapidly being replaced by the more rugged and manoeuvrable biplane fighter, so in an effort to stay in contention, Pfalz produced the Pfalz D.4. The fuselage of an E.V was taken and broadened, whilst the rudder assembly came from another of the E-series. The first version produced was an unmitigated disaster and was virtually uncontrollable. The second version had some modifications but didn't resolve the main problems. Only one of each was built.

At the end of 1916, with the E-series of monoplane aircraft completed, the Pfalz company was instructed to build the L.F.G. (*Luft-Fahrzeug-Gesellschaft*) Roland D.I under licence. Up to this point a total of 300 A and E-types of aircraft had been constructed by Pfalz. The reason that Pfalz had been asked to build the Roland, was because the Roland factory had been destroyed by fire and Pfalz had just completed building the last of their E-series of fighter/reconnaissance aircraft.

Pfalz D.III Scout.

During the period of constructing the L.F.G., the Pfalz design office were working on a design for a biplane fighter of their own. Then at the beginning of 1917, the first of the D-series of Pfalz aircraft appeared. This was a biplane version of the E.V monoplane and was given the name of *Walfisch* (Whale). This short, tubby little aircraft, thought to have been powered by a 100-hp Mercedes D.I engine with a car-type radiator at the nose, was unusual in that it had almost an enclosed cockpit. From information gathered, it appears that it was never designed as a fighter, but to be used for reconnaissance missions. It is not known how many were built, but it is thought that there were only two.

One aircraft that appeared at the beginning of 1917, was designated the Pfalz C.I. It was in reality a Rumpler C.IV, built under licence by the Pfalz company. It had additional bracing struts from the tailplane to the fin and ailerons on all four wingtips. Powered by a 260-hp Mercedes D.IVa engine, this two-seater reconnaissance aircraft was armed with one forward firing Spandau machine gun and one manually operated Parabellum machine gun mounted in the observers cockpit. The designation of the Rumpler C.IV as the Pfalz C.I was a perfect example of the rivalry that existed between the various states and principalities. The Bavarian leaders insisted on purchasing only Bavarian-built aircraft, so when Bavarian companies built aircraft from other states, which

Pfalz D.III being readied for a test flight from the Pfalz factory.

Pfalz D.III flown by Vzfw. Hecht of Jasta 10 *in R.F.C. markings after being brought down by 2/Lieutenants Hanna and Burnand of No. 35 Squadron, R.F.C.*

were given designations pertaining to Bavarian companies, the leaders felt justified in purchasing them. It was this petty minded thinking that hampered the flow of materials and aircraft to the Front.

By the summer of 1917 the first of the Pfalz fighters appeared, the Pfalz D.III. The fuselage was of a wooden semi-monocoque construction made up of spruce longerons and oval plywood formers. The fuselage was then wrapped with two

Pfalz D.III

layers of plywood strip in a spiral fashion in opposing directions, and then covered in fabric which was then painted with dope. The vertical tail fin was part of the main fuselage and made of fabric covered wood. The rounded rudder however was made of welded steel tube construction covered in fabric.

Powered by a six-cylinder, in-line, water-cooled Mercedes D.III engine which gave the D. III a top speed of 102 mph, a climb rate of almost 1,000 feet per minute and an operating ceiling of 17,000 feet with a duration of 2 1/2 hours. It was armed with two synchronised, forward firing Spandau machine-guns.

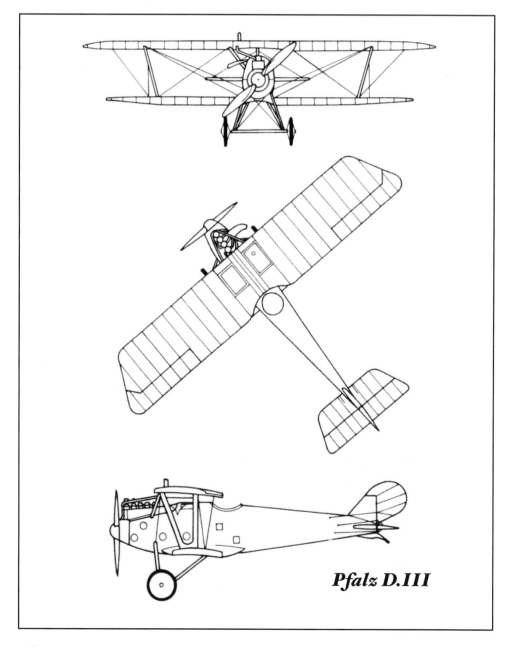

Pfalz D.III

Pfalz D.III Specifications

Performance

Wingspan: 30 ft. 9 ins. (9.4 m).
Length: 22 ft. 8 ins. (6.95 m).
Height: 8 ft. 7 ins. (2.67 m).
Weight Empty: 1,519 lb. (689 kg.).
Weight Loaded: 2,033 lb. (922 kg.).
Maximum speed: 102 mph.
Ceiling: 17,000 ft. Duration: 2 $^1/_2$ hours
Armament: Two synchronised forward-firing
Spandau machine-guns.
Engine: 160-hp Mercedes D.III inline

Pfalz D.VI

The Pfalz D.VI was the next in the series and was one of the most elegant of Pfalz aircraft. The fuselage was constructed with the now familiar wrapped strip plywood, which was then covered in fabric and painted with dope. Powered by a 110-hp Oberursel U.II rotary engine which was completely enclosed in a metal cowl. It had a wingspan of 23ft. 3in. and a top speed of 110 mph. No actual figures are available to the number built, but it is believed to have been around twenty.

Pfalz company test pilot Otto August with an unarmed Pfalz D.VI.

Leutnant *Frankl with his Pfalz D.VI.*

Shortly after the D.VI model was dispatched to the front, the Pfalz D.VII appeared. There were two versions of this aircraft, one with the 160-hp Siemens-Halske Sh.III geared rotary engine, the second was with a 160-hp Oberursel UR.III rotary engine. A third engine was also tried in the D.VII, the 160-hp Goebel Goe.III.

There were some slight differences in the dimension of each aircraft, the wingspan on the 1st. version was 24 ft 8 in. and 26 ft 7 in. on the second. The fuselage length on the first version was 18 ft 7 in., on the 2nd was 18 ft 3 in. Top speed for both aircraft was 118 mph and both were equipped with twin

Pfalz D.VII on its tail stand at the factory.

Leutnant der Reserve *Paul Bäumer of* Jasta Boelcke *walking toward his Pfalz D.VI fighter. Note the markings beneath the wings*

synchronised forward-firing Spandau machine guns.

At the same time as the D.VII was being constructed a tri-plane was being constructed. The Pfalz experimental triplane was a D.III conversion and fitted with a six-cylinder, in-line, water-cooled 160-hp Mercedes D.III engine. For some unknown reason it never flew and was scrapped. The information gained however was not lost and some months later came another triplane, the Pfalz Dr. I.

The Pfalz Dr.I was a stocky, powerful little aircraft with a wingspan of 28 ft 1 in. and a fuselage length of 18ft. It was powered with the 160-hp Siemens-Halske Sh.III rotary engine that gave it a top speed of 112 mph and a climb rate of

Head-on view of the Pfalz D.VII.

almost 1,500 feet per minute. Despite the powerful engine its performance rating was not as good as the Fokker Dr.Is and because of this less than ten were manufactured. In an attempt to find an improved version of the Pfalz Dr.I, the Dr.II and Dr.IIa were developed. These two aircraft were powered by the 110-hp Oberursel UR.II and 110-hp Siemens Sh.I respectively. Neither were successful and were not put into production.

Pfalz D.VIII

At the beginning of 1918, another single-seat fighter appeared, the Pfalz D.VIII. Three versions of this aircraft existed each powered by a different engine, a 160-hp Siemens-Halske Sh.III, a 160-hp Oberursel U.III and a Goebel Goe.III. Of the three variants only the Siemens-Halske engined model was manufactured in any number, forty being built. The aircraft had a wingspan of 24ft. 8in., a

Pfalz D.VIII on its tail stand..

fuselage length of 118ft. 6_in. and a height of 9ft. The Siemens-Halske powered model had a top speed of 112 mph and a climb rate of 1,200 feet per minute. Almost identical to the D.VII, the aircraft was sent to the Front line for evaluation with *Jagdstaffeln 5, 14* and *29*. Reports came back saying that although the aircraft was excellent to fly, its undercarriage had a tendency to collapse on landing. However, nineteen of the aircraft were still in operational service by the end of the year, but it never went into full production. Two modified versions were produced with different engines, but the confidence in the aircraft had gone and neither went into production.

One interesting experiment was carried out with the Pfalz D.VIII, using a Rhemag R.II engine which drove two counter-rotating propellers. On its first flight the aircraft crashed because it was excessively nose-heavy. The engine was then removed and repaired and shipped to Aldershof, Berlin to be fitted into a Siemens-Schuckert D.IV, but before the tests could begin the war came to an end and the project was scrapped.

Although the Pfalz company had produced a number of excellent aircraft, with the exception of the Pfalz D.III, none of them had been particularly successful. The only other model that came anywhere near the D.III, was the Pfalz D.XII.

Pfalz D.XII

Looking similar to the Fokker D.VII, the D.XII was of a semi-monocoque design, constructed of spruce longerons with plywood formers. The fuselage was then wrapped with two layers of thin plywood strip, applied in opposite directions, then covered in fabric and painted with dope. Powered by a 160-hp six-cylinder, in-line, water-cooled Mercedes D.IIIa engine with a `car type' radiator mounted on the front, the D.XII had a top speed of 112 mph, a climb rate of almost 1,000 feet per minute and an operating ceiling of 18,500 feet.

When the first production models were sent to the Front to replace the worn out Albatros D.Vas and Pfalz D.IIIs, some of Germany's top pilots, including *Oberleutnant* Ernst Udet and *Oberleutnant* Hans Weiss, flew the aircraft and declared it as good as, if not better in some regards, as the already established Fokker D.VII. The Bavarian *Jagdgeschwader IV*, commanded by *Oberleutnant* Eduard *Ritter* von Schleich reported that although initially his pilots did not

Ground crew working on a Pfalz D.XII with an armed guard watching over them.

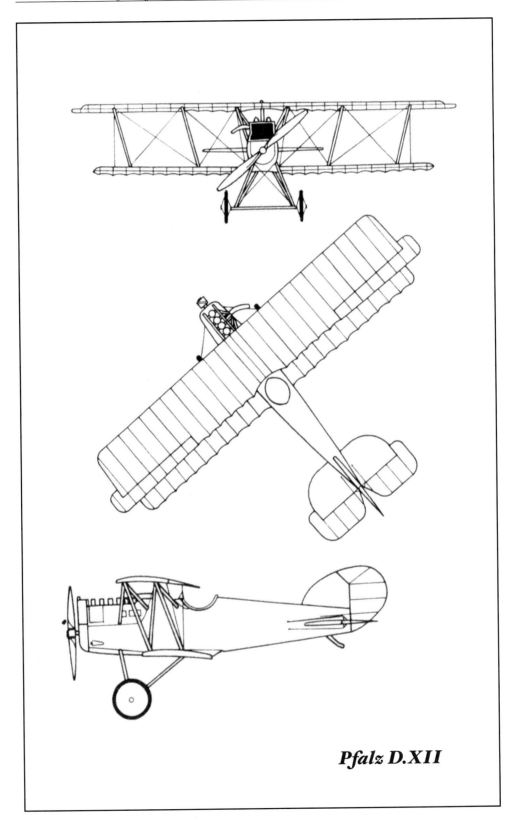

Pfalz D.XII

```
              Pfalz D.XII Specifications
         Performance

         Wingspan:          29 ft 6 ins. (9.0 m).
         Length:            20 ft 8 ins. (6.35 m).
         Height:            8 ft  8 ins. (2.70 m).
         Weight Empty:      1,569 lb. (712 kg.).
         Weight Loaded:     1,966 lb. (892 kg.).
         Maximum speed:     112 mph.
         Duration:          1 1/2 hours.
         Armament:          Two Synchronised forward-
                            firing Spandau machine-guns.
         Engine:            180-hp Mercedes DIIIa inline
```

look too favourably on the replacement aircraft, their opinion changed rapidly after they had flown them in combat.

Whether or not their recommendation carried any real weight, but more than 300 Pfalz D XIIs were supplied to *Jastas* 23, 32, 34, 35, 64, 65, 66, 77, 78 and 81. By the end of 1918 over 180 of the aircraft were still in operation on the Western Front.

Pfalz D.IIIa

Later in 1918 an improved model, the Pfalz D.IIIa appeared. It had an improved engine, the 180-hp Mercedes D.IIIa, the tailplane area had been increased and a modification to the wingtips of the lower wing. In all other areas it was the same as the D.III model. In all over 800 of the Pfalz D.III and D.IIIa were built and according to the Inter-Allied Control Commissions figures at least 350 were still operational on the Front line at the end of the war. It was without question the most successful fighter produced by the Pfalz factory.

Whilst still continuing to upgrade their existing aircraft, Pfalz produced an experimental model, the Pfalz D.XIV. Slightly larger than the D.XII it had a larger vertical fin and was powered by a 200-hp Benz Bz.IVü engine. This gave the aircraft a top speed of 113 mph and a climb rate of just over 1,000 feet per minute. Only the one was built.

The results gained from this aircraft resulted in the production of the last of the single-seat fighters, the Pfalz D.XV. Its first official test flight was on November 4, 1918 and 180 were ordered. It is not known how many were actually built, but it is unlikely to have been the full complement, bearing in mind the Armistice came a week later. The D.XV was powered by a 180-hp Mercedes D.IIIa engine, there were a number of models that were fitted with the 185-hp BMW IIIa engine, which

Pfalz D.IIIa.

gave the aircraft a top speed of 125 mph. The aircraft had a wingspan of 28 ft 3 in., a fuselage length of 21 ft 4 in. and a height of 8 ft 10 in.

Like a number of German aircraft, the Pfalz became one of the most respected fighter aircraft of the First World War by both its pilots and by its opponents.

Pfalz D.IIIa Specifications

Performance

Wingspan:	36 ft 7 ins. (11.2 m).
Length:	23 ft 2 ins. (7.06 m).
Height:	8 ft 8 ins. (2.68 m).
Weight Empty:	1,532 lb. (695 kg.).
Weight Loaded:	2.017 lb. (915 kg.).
Maximum speed:	113 mph.
Duration:	2 hours.
Armament:	Two Synchronised forward-firing Spandau machine-guns.
Engine:	180-hp Mercedes DIIIa.

CHAPTER FIVE

Sopwith 7F-1 Snipe

It was early morning of October 2, 1918, and the Great War was in its final stages, but the ground and air battles continued with ferocity. One of the latest Sopwith fighters to enter service with the Royal Air Force, the Snipe, in the colours No. 21 Squadron, Royal Air Force, was flying over the French landscape when it encountered a Fokker two-seat reconnaissance aeroplane.

The British fighter attacked and the German aircraft fell to earth. Unseen to the pilot a Fokker D.VII appeared from below and in the mêlée the British pilot was wounded. Losing height rapidly the British fighter encountered a large formation of enemy aircraft.

Immediately one was shot down in flames, and the Canadian pilot turned his attention to the rest of the formation. He was wounded in his thigh, and the enemy pilots watched as the Snipe spun out of control. As it passed through yet another enemy formation the pilot shot one down in flames for his third victory.

He had been wounded twice and could scarcely control his fighter, which he managed to level out at around 12,000 feet, only to face more of the enemy. In

Snipe 7.F1/5 B9966 with 200-hp Bentley engine.

a last effort to escape from the surrounding Fokker D.VIIs he managed to shoot down his fourth and dive away to crash land behind the Allied front lines.

The pilot was Major W.G.Barker, a Canadian, and for his magnificent victory he was awarded the Victoria Cross. His mount was the final Sopwith fighter design to serve in World War Two, the Snipe. It was this episode that brought the Snipe to the attention of the British and Canadian people.

In the summer of 1917 squadrons of the R.A.F. had taken delivery of a new Sopwith biplane scout called the Camel. This aeroplane was to have a marked effect on the fortunes of the R.A.F., and it continued in service until the end of the war. Its successor was already in production but only small numbers were available before the war ended.

The Camel replacement was the Sopwith Snipe and it was in design and concept an updated Camel. It was in April 1917 that the British Air Board was to issue the specification for an aeroplane that was to succeed the Camel. Specification A.1(a) asked for submissions for the design and development of a single seat, tractor aeroplane which would have two synchronised machine-guns firing through the propeller disc. Ammunition was specified as 750 rounds for the forward-firing guns, and 250 rounds for the pivoted gun installed on top of the upper centre wing section. Additional items were oxygen apparatus, armour plating for pilot protection, a speed of not less than 135 mph at 15,000 ft and a ceiling of 25,000 ft. The maximum speed of the Camel at 15,000 ft was approximately 111 mph.

The requirements of the performance specification appeared too high for the available power plants of the period, but the Air Board had anticipated the need

7.F1 Snipe, first prototype.

for a larger engine when, in the same month, it ordered three examples of a new engine designed by Lieutenant W.O.Bentley. It was the B.R.2, and enlarged development of the reliable B.R.1. The new design was 93 lbs heavier than the B.R.1, 1082 mm in diameter and 1131 mm in length.

The Sopwith company was actively engaged in designing the Camel replacement, and one of the first drawings of the 7F-1 Snipe appeared on August 14, 1917. It revealed a larger aeroplane but still powered by the standard Camel engines- the B.R.1 (150-hp); Gnôme Monosoupape (150-hp); Clerget 9B (110-hp and 130-hp) and the Le Rhône (110-hp). A large spinner was proposed, but abandoned due to cooling problems.

To speed development of the Snipe the Air Board placed a contract (British Requisition No. 224) with Sopwith for the construction of six prototypes, serial numbers B9962 to 9967. A formal contract, AS31668, followed on October 31. Due to an error in the ordering system an order had already been placed almost three weeks previously for 300 production aircraft, thus pre-empting the order for the six prototypes on the 31st. In the event the serial numbers for the prototypes were confirmed on November 10, 1917 some seven days after the premature contract.

By the time Sopwith had reported to a Progress and Allocation Committee on 1 November that the first prototype was undergoing trials at the company's Brooklands airfield, and delivery of the other five airframes would follow in approximately three weeks. Prototype B9963 was delivered to Farnborough on

Snipe, serial number of B9963.

23 November with the third machine being modified for installation of the ABC Dragonfly engine.

Progress with airframe and engine was proceeding at and accelerated pace and such was the considered potential of the engine that one member of the Air Board suggested it be used in all single seat aeroplanes in production.

7.F1 first prototype Snipe in its second form with 150-hp. Bentley BR.1 engine.

The first example was bench tested in October 1917, producing 234-hp, and the Air Board drew up plans for the production of 1500 units per calendar month. Confirmed orders for 900 engines were placed a few weeks later.

Prototype Snipe was completed at approximately the same time as the B.R.2 was under test, and it bore a strong resemblance to its smaller predecessor, having short, equal span wings with single bay bracing. To ease quantity production, the designers had incorporated the fin and rudder of the Camel, and this unit was taken from a production Camel and installed on the prototype. The airframe was ready for trials before a B.R.2 was available, and it was decided to flight test it with a 150-hp B.R.1.

Maker's trials were quickly completed, and the prototype delivered to Farnborough on 23 November 1917. Official trials commenced the following month at Martlesham Heath. A second prototype (B9963) followed and it incorporated a number of modifications, including a wider, upper wing centre section; the centre section struts were lengthened and splayed outwards. Also, the centre section trailing edge was cut away to improve pilot's view. Fuselage stringers were lengthened to fair the rear fuselage into the final vertical spacer. These two prototypes had single bay wings, but trials had

Snipe with single bay wings and 200-hp. BR.2 engine.

suggested they needed strengthening.

The third prototype appeared in January 1918 with a two bay, wider span (increased by 4 ft 3 in) wings of 30 ft span, and the original fin and rudder. Martlesham Reports, Numbers M.176 and M.176A (February 1918), and M.176B (April 1918) revealed a loss of performance, due to an increase in weight brought about by the wider wing structure and an increased armament. Twin Vickers.303 inch machine-guns were fitted to prototype two, but the third machine had the centre-section mounted Lewis. This mounting was to be criticised in the Martlesham Reports, which stated 'The Lewis gun, as at present mounted, is practically impossible for the pilot to operate so close is it located to his head'. The Vickers guns were accepted as good, and flying characteristics were variable.

Engine torque on take off was fierce when the B.R.2 was installed, and from the fourth prototype the fin and rudders was progressively increased in area. With completion of the first series of Martlesham trials, B9965, on February 23, 1918, the aeroplane was despatched to France for operational evaluation, arriving at No. 1 Aeroplane Supply Depot on March 13. Pilot reports were favourable and the Snipe considered to be, 'Vastly superior to any scout at the front. Manoeuvrable, easy and slow to land'. A different opinion to that of Martlesham Heath. On return to England B9965 had a large spinner fitted, plus a modified cowling. It was returned to Martlesham for intensive flying trials; transferred to Farnborough in July.

The fifth prototype, B9966, had horn balanced ailerons on the upper wings and a redesigned, enlarged, tail unit. The tail was sharply tapered in plan

Snipe, serial B9966.

form with broad chord root. The fin now blended in to the rudder resulting in an oval shaped unit. The tailplane was adjustable in flight by means of a mechanism actuated by a handle in the cockpit. This Snipe carried the designation of 7F.1/5 and it went to Martlesham Heath in June 1918, at almost the same moment that large scale production was launched.

The final Snipe prototype was B9967, and it differed from the first five in having a 320-hp A.B.C Dragonfly engine of nine cylinders. Construction was finished in April 1918 and, following maker's trials it was delivered to Farnborough on the 11th of May. Its length had been increased by 1 ft 10 in., but it still had the small fin and rudder, and possessed a maximum speed of 156 mph.

Although progress with service trials had produced some good results

Snipe lacks serial number and is probably a new production aircraft. 200-hp Bentley rotary engine.

there were a number of adverse comments about the Snipe's performance. A report of February 22, 1918 stated that performance was below requirements in that a maximum speed at 15,000 ft was 20 mph less than the required 130. Range was restricted due to insufficient fuel, and the amount of ammunition was 300 rounds less than what had been specified.

All round performance was heavily criticised and Sopwith ordered to correct the faults outlined in the Report, part of which stated; 'This machine as it stands is unsuitable for adoption as a type'. However, General Trenchard, General-Officer-Commanding, was impressed after a field demonstration and said the Snipe was the aircraft required for service.

The Dragonfly powered variant

For reasons known only to the Air Board the decision was taken to produce a Dragonfly engined Snipe with the new name of Dragon. As related above the final Snipe prototype, B9967, had an early production Dragonfly engine installed in April 1918 and it lengthened the fuselage by 22 inches. One normal production Snipe, E7990, became the prototype Dragon, when fitted with a Dragonfly in January 1919. It also had the longer fuselage, but had adopted the new, enlarged fin and rudder. It had been intended to despatch this aeroplane to America as a pattern aircraft for possible production, but it was never delivered. However, Dragon J3628 was delivered to the McCook test airfield in July 1921 and it was fitted with the 400-hp Liberty 12 engine. Trials Reports were critical of the Dragon's performance.

Swnipe powered by A.B.C. Dragonfly engine. E7990.

Front view of the Snipe with Dragonfly engine.

The Dragon had a much superior all round performance to the Snipe but one serious fault. The new engine was unreliable. Despite this a Contract No. 35 A/1440/C1520 for production of Dragons F7001 to 7030 was placed with Sopwith on June 3, 1918. A second batch, J3617 to 3916 was ordered and deliveries started in June 1919 but only a small proportion were delivered. A two-seat Dragon was designed in April 1920 but never proceeded with. Also a naval version for shipboard use was under preparation, and plans had been laid to equip the Home Defence Squadrons The Dragon was officially declared obsolete in April 1923.

A third engine specified for the Snipe was the Clerget 11Eb, eleven cylinder delivering 200-hp. One was installed in F2340 and the aeroplane delivered to Farnborough on January 1, 1919.

The Snipe had been selected for large-scale production in preference to the competitive Boulton & Paul Bobolink, Nieuport B.N.1. and Sopwith Snail. Seven contracts, dated March 20, 1918, for a total of 1,800 Snipes were allotted as follows;

Manufacturer.	Contract No.	Serial Nos
Sopwith	35A/432/C300	E7001-E7030*,
		E7987-E8286,
		F2333-F2532
		H4865-H5064,
		J3617-J3916**
Barclay, Curle	Cancelled	J3917-J3991+

Boulton & Paul	35A/436/C303	E6137-E6536
J451-JJ550+		
British Caudron	Cancelled	J651-JJ680,
		J2392-J2541+
Coventry Ordnance Works	35A/437/C304	E6537-E668
		F9846-F9995+
Gloucestershire A/C Co		J3042-J3341
Grahame-White Aviation		J2542-J3041
Kingsbury Aviation		J6493-J6522+
March, Jone and Cribb		J301-J400,
		J681-J730
Napier & Son	35A/434/C302	E6787-E6936
National & General AC		E6787-EE6936+
Nieuport & General	35A/435/C305	E6937-E7036
		H8513-H8662#
Porthholme Aerodrome	35A/431/C299	E8307-E8406,
		H8663-H8762+
Ruston Proctor	35A/433/C301	E7337-E7836
		H351-H650+

** Ordered as Snipes but delivered as Dragons. ** Ordered as Snipes, production as Dragons. +
Cancelled. # Built as Nighthawk.*

By December 1918 497 aircraft been delivered. The R.A.F. had planned to equip eight Night Fighter Squadrons and eleven squadrons stationed in France, with aircraft fitted with Dragonfly engines. In addition 22 aircraft, with the more reliable ABC engine, were to be supplied with a target date of May 1919. The cost of the airframe, without the engine, instruments and guns, was £945.17s. The engine, £880. A grand total of 4515 Snipes were ordered and at least 1567 production examples completed.

By the summer of 1918 a small number of Snipes had been delivered. The first Sopwith production aircraft, E7987, was sent to Martlesham and the official trial report No. M.223, of August, was critical. 'With an engine specially tuned to deliver 245-hp performance was just comparable with that of B9965, and this had the additional load and drag of its Lewis gun'.

The Lewis was abandoned for the production Snipe, and subsequent production aircraft were different to the prototypes. A new, larger rudder was fitted and the cut-out in the centre section was enlarged. Internally, a number of structural members were altered; the design of several fittings improved, and an enlarged combined gravity and oil tank of revised shape was fitted behind the engine. Oxygen equipment and electrical heating apparatus were standard

Snipe, probably served with No. 1 Squadron.

fittings. By the end of September 1918 a total of 161 Snipes had passed final inspection.

A second version of the Snipe was produced when the Independent Force, R.A.F., required a long-range fighter. The Martinsyde was the preferred choice but it was still in the design/prototype stages. Sopwith created the Snipe 1a which had a 50-gallon fuel tank installed under the pilot's seat and other minor

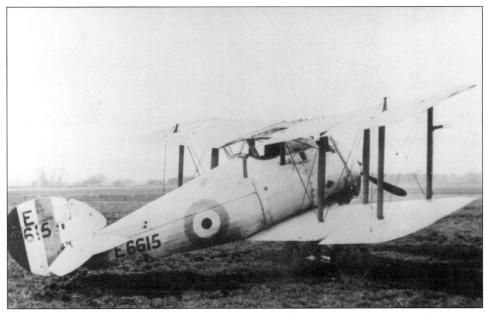

Snipe E6615. Of No. 23 Squadron. Also served with Central Flying School.

changes.

The first prototype was E8089 which was completed by September 18, 1918 and at one time it had a Dolphin tail unit. Two more prototypes followed, E8090 to E8091. By the end of the month all three aircraft had a change of serial number to H9964 to H9966. The prototypes were followed by an order for 50 production examples, E8211 to E8260, and they were rejected for service as airframe faults restricted anything except normal flying.

Production of the Snipe was expanded in the summer of 1918 with additional orders for 200 machines (F2333 to F2532) placed with Sopwith. These were followed by H4865 to H5064. Contracts were also placed for 900 machines in the autumn. The Armistice resulted in cancellations with batches J451 to J550, H351 to H650 and E7337 to E7836. Production by outside contractors ended on January 29, 1919, and Sopwith built the final Snipe on 1 March 1919.

American Snipe. Note the Indian head on rudder.

Very few Snipes were delivered to France, and by October 17, 1918, just 97 examples had arrived. When the Armistice was declared only three squadrons had been equipped. The first unit was No. 43 Squadron, R.A.F. followed by No..4 of the Australian Flying Corps. In October No. 208 Squadron had exchanged its Camels for the new type. No. 43 made its first operational sortie with its new aircraft on September 23, 1918, and during the final seven weeks of war No. 43 was used as an escort squadron, notably to the D.H.9s of No. 107 Squadron.

The Snipes of No. 4 Squadron, Australian Flying Corps, fought off fifteen Fokkers near Tournai on October 26. On the 30th, as part of the 80th Wing attack on an enemy base at Rebaix, No. 4's Snipes destroyed six Fokkers of an enemy flight. As they returned to base the Australians shot up enemy ground transport.

Sopwith Snipe of the Central Flying School.

No. 208 Squadron, R.A.F., also took delivery of the new Sopwith in October 1918, but the war ended before the squadron never used its machines operationally.

The majority of Sopwith Camel squadrons were re-equipped with Snipes as from January 1919. It took part in trials as a night fighter and was declared to be suitable. The Independent Air Force wanted a long-range Snipe, and this was supplied for use as an escort for Force's bombers. It carried the designation 7F.1a, and had a special fuel tank installed under the pilot's seat. With this additional fuel the long-range version had an endurance of 4 ¹/2 hours. The official flight test report of the Snipe, Mark IA was dated November 1918. A number of Home defence squadrons took delivery of the Snipe, including Nos. 37, 78, 112 and 143. Known R.A.F. Squadrons to use the Snipe were Nos. 1, 3, 14, 17, 19, 23, 25, 29, 32, 41, 43, 45, 56, 71, 80, 81, 111, 112, 201 and 208.

No. 43 Squadron and No. 4 A.F.C. were stationed in Bickendorf, Germany, as part of the Army of Occupation. One Snipe was flown to Russia.

The Navy was interested in the Snipe and two machines, E8111 and 8112, were allocated for trials. E8068 was fitted with an hydrovane and wheels capable of being jettisoned to prevent overturning when ditching. Trials took

Snipe, serial number of F2453.

place in May 1919. E8085 was fitted with slinging and floatation gear in July, and several years after official trials has ceased, E6611 was fitted with deck-landing arrester gear.

A Sopwith-built production Snipe fitted with a Sopwith Dolphin tail assembly was also flown at Martlesham. E8137 was fitted with the Calthrop A.1 parachute.

A two-seat version of the Snipe, for training purposes, was designed by Sopwith in 1919, with the second cockpit situated immediately behind the first. No armament was fitted, and the majority of squadrons had one example on station. A total of approximately 40 Snipe were converted and conversions of the Dragon were on order.

There were examples of Snipes on the Civil register, including - G-EAUU (J459), G-EAUV (J453), G-EAUW (J455). All were entered for the 1920 Aerial Derby on 24th July.

Leading Particulars. First prototype

Dimensions. Wing span: 25 ft 9 in. Area: 230 sq. ft. Chord: 5 ft 0 in. Ailerons: 38 sq. ft. Gap: 4 ft 3 in. Stagger: 1 ft 5 in. Dihedral: 2º 30min. Incidence: 2º. Tailplane span: 8 ft 0 in. Area: 14 sq. ft. Elevators: 5 sq. ft. Fin area: 3 sq. ft.

Rudder 4.9 sq. ft. Length 18ft.11in. Height 8ft.3in. Engine one x 150-hp Bentley BR1 or one x 230-hp. Bentley BR2. Weights. Tare 1153 lb. Auw 1674 lb. Performance. Maximum speed at 15,000ft 119mph. Climb to 6500ft. 4min.10secs. To 15,000ft 14min.50sec. Service ceiling 21.500ft. Endurance. Not known. Fuel. 38.5 gals. Oil 7 gals. Three prototypes were constructed and all varied in leading particulars.

Production aircraft

Dimensions. Wing span (Top) 31ft.0in. (Lower) 30ft.0in. 271 sq. ft. Chord 5ft.0in. Ailerons 40 sq. ft. Gap 4ft 3in. Stagger 1ft 4in. Dihedral 4°.

Incidence 1° 50min. Tailplane span 9ft 2in. Area 15 sq. ft. Elevator area 2.75 sq. ft. Fin area 2.75 sq. ft. Rudder 9 sq. ft. Length 19ft 10in. Height 9ft 6in. Wheel track 5ft.0in. Engine one x 230-hp Bentley BR2. Fuel 38.5gals. Weights. Tare 1312 lb. Auw 2020 lb. Performance. Maximum speed at 15,000ft. 113mph. At 10,000ft, 121.Climb to 5000ft in 3min.45secs. To 10,000ft., 9min.25secs. To 15,000ft 18min.50sec. Service ceiling 19,500ft. Endurance. 3 hours. Armament. two fixed, forward firing .303in. Vickers machine guns firing through propeller. Four x 25 lb. bombs could also be carried.

Two-seat variant of the Snipe, E6531, of No. 3 Squadron seen at the C.F.S., Upavon, 1925.

Camouflage markings

The majority of Snipes left the Sopwith factory with a clear Cellon dope applied overall. Upper flying surfaces and fuselage were in P10 khaki dope. Engine cowling and metal panels to the rear of the engine were in a Sea Grey. Most wooden assembled such as the interplane struts and undercarriage oleos were plain varnished. National markings had a coat of clear varnish. Wheel covers varied and were seen with flight colours, red, white and blue. Squadron colours were applied during the 1920s.

Production example of the Snipe 7.F1, August 1918.

Sopwith 7.F1 Snipe

CHAPTER SIX

The Caproni Biplane Giants

When Italy entered the war in 1916 to become an Ally of France and Great Britain, it had a thriving aviation industry which had produced a number of successful military aeroplanes. One of the many companies was the well-known Caproni Company, with works at Talido and offices in Milan, which was to develop a line of large, multi-engined biplane bombers.

The Company was founded in 1911 and concentrated on building aeroplanes that were contemporary with current practices. However, within a few months the company was in grave financial trouble and eventually due to the need for fighting aeroplanes in 1914 the Italian Government purchased the Caproni works and placed orders for various types of biplanes, including the well known giant bombers.

The first order was for twelve bombers known as the Ca.1, Ca.300 and Ca. 350, the last two names referred to the engine power with which the aircraft was fitted such as the Fiat A.10 of 100-hp (three engines).

The first production of the Ca.1 were powered by two 100-hp Fiat A.10 in-line engines. Gianni Caproni (left) is shown handing over the aircraft to the Italian Aero Service, August 1915.

A second order soon followed for 150 aircraft called the Ca.2 (Ca.350) in January 1916 and a number were used for flight testing various engines and weapon systems. There followed the Ca. 3 (or Ca.450) powered by three x 150-hp. Isotta-Fraschini V.4Bs. These were used for mass bombing attacks against Austria with up to 36 bombers taking part. They were also used as ground attack aircraft against enemy ground forces and other military installations.

The company was chosen by America when it entered the First World War to supply bombers to the Allied nations with America being responsible for funding the whole programme. The reasoning behind this decision was due to America having insufficient aeroplanes and having to catch up with the British and French and German Air Forces as it lacked aeroplanes, in particular bombers. Also, when the Company entered into an agreement with the American Air Force, it also agreed to train and employ in Italy large numbers of fledging American pilots.

Ca.3 powered by three 150-hp Isotta Frachini V4B in-line engines. The version shown was also known as the Ca.450.

The National Defence Act of 1916 increased the strength of the American Aviation section and established a reserve corps of officers and enlisted men. Plans for further expansion did not mature fast enough and at the outbreak of war the American Army Air Force had 20 squadrons on paper. The American Congress was to vote the sum of £540M for the purchase of aircraft and funding of a total of 345 squadrons, 45 construction companies, 81 supply and 11 repair squadrons.

The President signed the Act on July 24, 1917, and aircraft production was established as 22,635, plus 44,000 engines and 80% spare parts per annum. Of this total 12,000 were earmarked for France at a time when there was just 12 companies capable of producing aeroplanes in America. Total production for the previous year was less than 400. It was a sorry state of affairs and despite America's production capacity there was not sufficient time in which to meet this enormous programme.

The number of squadrons had to be reduced to 202 of which 41 were to be bombardment. The training programme for recruiting and training of 38,000 volunteer pilots, 58,000 officers and men was established.

Due to this enormous proposal America had to turn to its new Allies, and in June 1917 had sent a large mission, the Bolling Mission, consisting of technicians and politicians to Europe to negotiate with European manufacturers to acquire licence rights to build aircraft, or have them supplied by European companies and distributed to the Allied Forces in Europe. In the August of that year France agreed to produce 6000 aircraft plus 8500 engines, and eventually a total of nine types were chosen. Almost 6000 aircraft were delivered to the American Expeditionary Force in France during 1918, of which only 1200 were American built, the Curtiss-built de Havilland D.H.4.

This event had taken place after discussions with America that Curtiss would also built the reconnaissance bomber, the Handley Page giant and Italian Caproni bombers, and it the latter that this narrative details.

The Caproni Company agreed to supply a number of their designs which

Under normal conditions the Ca.3 lifted off after 150 metres.

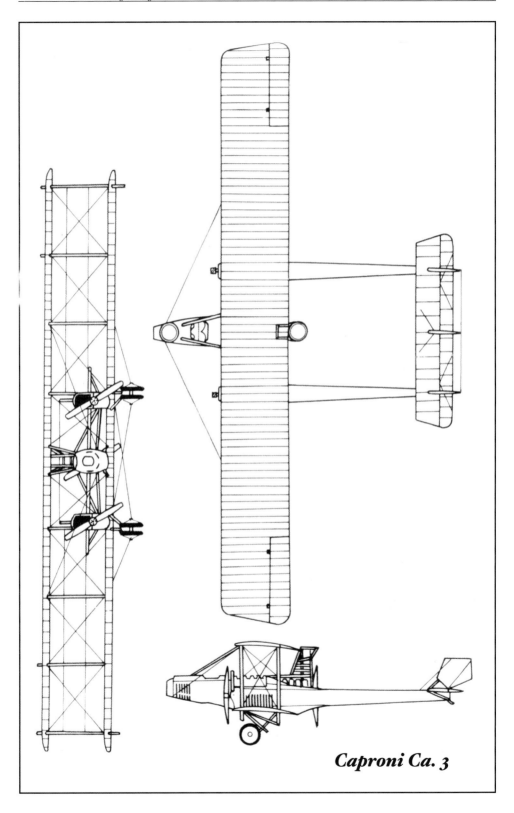

Caproni Ca. 3

were to prove unsuccessful. Initial orders had been placed for 50 to be built by Standard Aircraft, 500 by Curtiss and 500 by the Fisher Body Corporation. It also envisaged that 5000 were to be built in France and Italy.

Caproni's contribution to the Allied Bomber Force

The Army Air Service decided to built three of the Caproni giant bomber. The twin-engined Ca.3 (Models Ca.33, 34, 35 and 36), the three 150-hp engined Ca.4 (Ca.40, 41 and 42) and the Ca.5 (Model Ca.44, 45 and 46), all with engines of 200-hp with the exception of the Ca.4. However, it proved to be a wrong decision as not only were the bombers lacking performance, Caproni executives proved difficult to work with and insisted there would be no changes made to the original designs.

The average cost of each bomber was estimated at $15,000. The first American-built Caproni flew on July 4, 1919, and when the war ended the following November Standard Aircraft had delivered just two examples and Fisher Bodies three.

The Caproni team had arrived in America on August 28, 1917, to establish an American subsidiary and had also imported one Model Ca.33 biplane. The twin boom fuselage had two engines installed in the front sections plus a third at the rear end of the central nacelle. They were 150-hp. Isotta-Fraschini V-4-B engines. The main undercarriage was two sets of four wheels under the lower wing. The Americans called it 'The Caproni Triplane Bomber Sample'.

One of the first Caproni bombers to be exported to the United States. Here American student pilots familiarize themselves with the new machine.

The Sample bomber as readied for flight tests on 11 September and made a successful first flight followed by further flights during the following weeks. The Italian Air Force had 260 aircraft serving with 26 squadrons, plus one with the Navy. Licence production by the French Esnault-Pelerie Company enabled two *Escadrilles* of the *Aviation Militaire* to be equipped.

The Ca.34 lacked the nose-wheel undercarriage, square section fuselage and side by side seats for the two pilots. as the aircraft had an oval section, rather than square, fuselage and tandem seats. The Ca.36 had a detachable outer wing sections while the Ca.36S was converted for the ambulance role, the Ca.37 with shorter span wings and the Ca.39, a seaplane project.

Leading particulars, Ca.3 (Ca.33), Sample Bomber

Wing span: 72 ft 9 in. Length: 35 ft 9 in. Height: 12 ft 2 in. Weights, tare: 5400 lbs, gross: 7620. Max speed: 90mph. Engines: three x 150-hp Isotta-Fraschini Type V-4-B water cooled in line. Crew of three. Armament: one x Revilli machine-gun or cannon. Total production of 260 for the *Corpo Aeronautica Militaire.*

This list records only the variants mentioned above. Before the Ca.3 the Caproni Company had produced the Ca.30 of 1913 with central nacelle and twin booms. Engines were two x 80-hp. Gnome rotaries. The Ca.31, also a twin boom design powered by two Gnome engines. The Ca.2 (or Ca.32) of similar twin boom design and powered by three Fiat engines of 100-hp. Total of 160 built.

Ca.3. First model. Similar configuration to the Ca.2 (Ca.32) with a three bay biplane wing and twin-boom fuselage, plus central nacelle. Crew of three. Engines three x 150-hp. Isotta-Fraschini V-4-Bs. Total of 269 plus American prototypes.

Ca.34. Ca.3 variant and side by side pilots. Triple fin/rudder assembly and single tailplane and lacked nose-wheel undercarriage. Called the *'Guilio Cesare'*.

A Ca.37 'pusher' type that could reach speeds of up to 165 km/hr.

Ca.35. Ca.3 with oval section fuselage and tandem pilot positions.

Ca.36. Ca.3 with detachable outer panel wing sections.

Ca.36S. Ambulance version of the Ca.3.

Ca.37. Ca.3 Model with reduced span wings.

Ca.39. Proposed seaplane development of the Ca.3 with single, central float.

A second Caproni bomber had also been imported, the Ca.4 (Ca.42) triplane, an odd design with one wing above the fuselage, the second level with it and the third underneath. With a height of 20 feet it appeared to be an unsteady mount and was driven by three 270-hp Isotta-Fraschini water cooled engines driving propellers installed in the forward section of the twin booms, with a third at the rear of the central fuselage nacelle. The undercarriage installation consisted of two x eight wheel units.

Contemporary reports state this aeroplane made its first flight in America on December 1, 1917, and it had barely lifted off the ground when one engine stopped and the aeroplane dived into the ground to be totally destroyed. The American contract was for 1000 examples, later revised to 500, to be produced in France. In the event the contract was cancelled and a revised one placed for 1000 aircraft for the American Air Force and 2000 for Italy, all to be powered by Liberty engines. The Curtiss Company had a contract for 500 examples with the Liberty engines, and at a cost of $15,000 per completed airframe. Only three prototypes were constructed but no production ordered.

In 1916 Cparoni produced the Ca.4 – an enormous triplane powered by three Fiat A.12bis engines.

Leading particulars, Ca.4 (Ca.42)

Wing span: 98 ft 11 in., gap: 8 ft 0 in., chord: 7 ft 0 in., area 2223 sq.ft. Length: 49 ft 7 in. Height: 20 ft 8 in. Disposal weight: 3800 lbs, gross: 16,535. Max speed: 87 mph @ 6500 ft. Ceiling: 9843 ft. Climb to 6500 feet in 14 mins. Endurance: 7 hrs. Engines: three x Isotta-Fraschini water cooled 'V' in line. Propellers: two-bladed. Crew of two pilots and one gunner, the latter being, supposedly, accommodated in a pod situated behind the upper wing trailing edge. In some examples of the design a box-like carrier was installed over the main undercarriage.

Ca.4. Large, ungainly triplane of 1917, also built in America as prototypes. Side by side seating for the pilots plus front gunner cockpit and two positions in the booms immediately aft of the wing trailing edges. Retained Caproni twin boom configuration. Three x 200-hp Isotta-Fraschini engines. Aircraft lacked power.

The Ca.40 had an angular fuselage with clear sections in the nose for the observer.

Ca.40. Improved model of the basic Ca.4.

Ca.41. Twelve Ca.4 models constructed during 1918 with the more powerful 270-hp Isotta-Fraschini F engines. Oval centre section nacelle with tandem cockpits for pilots. Service with the Italian Army Air Force and Navy.

The six Liberty engines triplane, the Ca.42, was briefly operated by the Royal Naval Air Service.

Ca.42. Ca.4 model which could be regarded as the major production variant with 12 delivered. Six to British Royal Navy for service in 1918 but hastily withdrawn and returned to Italy. Powerplants were the Fiat, Isotta-Fraschini F or Liberty engines. Side by side seating for pilots. Square container suspended between the main undercarriage wheels for carriage of bombs (3,197 lbs) but doubtful is this total every carried. Used on night bombing raids.

A Liberty powered Ca.5 clearly showing the 'boxed' nacelle and the side mounted radiators.

Caproni Ca.5 (Ca.44, 45)

The most successful of the Caproni giants was the Ca.5 (Ca.44 to 47), of purposeful and elegant design of a biplane configuration. The first Model was the Ca.44 with two engines mounted on the front end of the twin boom fuselage, and one at the rear end of the central nacelle. The third design, a pusher, was situated at the rear end of the central nacelle. The Caproni-produced aircraft had an oval section central nacelle as did the American Standard and Fisher Body variants. A second model, the Ca.45, had a square section nacelle and was built by Standard in 1918/19, powered by Liberty engines.

One American-built aeroplane had a large boat (sled) installed between the undercarriage struts and filled with high explosive. The aircraft would tow the sled on the water's surface to a specified distance from the intended target, the sled was released to continue under its own momentum to the target while the carried Ca.5 increased speed and lifted off.

The Ca.44 entered service in Spring 1918 and was followed by the improved Ca.45 with Isotta-Fraschine engines. The next variant, the Ca.46, could be powered by the Fiat, Isotta-Fraschini or Liberty engine. The Ca.47 was a torpedo-bomber floatplane equipped with twin Zari floats and powered by Liberty engines. Piaggio was a main contractor and built ten examples delivered after the war had ended. The Ca.50 was the night bomber variant and took part in missions from French airfields. The total production run amounted to 255 examples, this not including American production.

The six Liberty engines triplane, the Ca.42, was briefly operated by the Royal Naval Air Service.

The Ca.5 had two 250-hp Isotta Fraschini V.6 engines. This variation was also known as the Ca.45.

The American prototypes were seen to be successful and America had to produce its own designs after the war and rarely purchased overseas models.

Leading particulars, Ca.5 (Ca.44 to 47)

Wing span: 76 ft 3 in., area: 1420 sq.ft, chord: 9 ft 1 in., gap: 9 ft 1 in. Length: 41 ft 2 in. Height: 12 ft 1 in. Weights, tare: 7700 lbs, gross: 12,094. Max speed @ S/L 98 mph. Ceiling 11,500 ft, climb to 6500 ft in 16 mins. Range: 250 miles (approx.). Engines: three x 300-hp. Fiat A-12*bis,* or 200/250-hp Isotta-Fraschini or, 330-hp. (@1600rpm) Liberty 12-N (CA.44 for Navy). Fuel: 45 gals. Armament: two defensive machine-guns plus 1800 lb. bombs. American built aircraft had three x .303 in Lewis machine-guns in nose section ahead of the pilots, who sat side by side, and two over the rear central nacelle as shown in drawings.

Ca.5. Biplane bomber of which the first model was the Ca.44 with three Fiat 200/300-hp engines. The wing mounted pair had frontal radiators. Two machine guns for defence and 1190 lb. bombs.

Ca.45. Ca.4 design improved with three x 200/250-hp Isotta-Fraschini engines.

Ca.46. Ca.4 Model which could accommodate either Fiat, Isotta-Fraschini or Liberty 12 engines.

Ca.5. Major production model with 255 built, plus batch by Esnault-Pelterie company in France. Three (Ca.46) exported to America and five prototypes built by Standard and Fisher Body companies.

Ca.47. Civil model with room for 30 passengers. Breda built a VIP model with seating for eight.

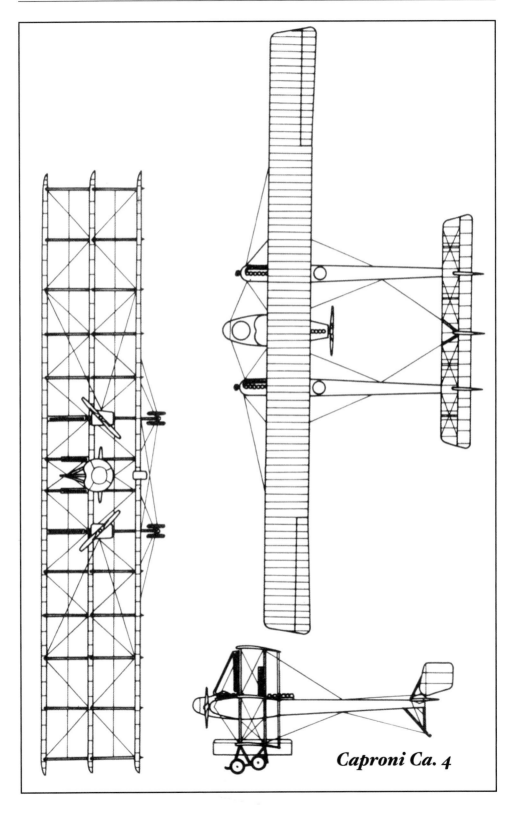

Caproni Ca. 4

CHAPTER SEVEN

LFG Roland

The company *Luftfahrzeug Gesellschaft* (LFG) had its roots back in 1906, when a company by the name of *Motorluftschiff Studiengesellschaft* had been created at the instigation of Kaiser Wilhelm II, to carry out the manufacture of airships. The company changed its name a few years later to LFG *Bitterfeld* from which sprang another company by the name of *Flugmaschine Wright GmbH*. Formed in 1909, the company was set up to develop some of the Wright Brothers patents, but never went into full production. Two years later, in 1912, the German courts declared the Wright Brothers patents void forcing the company into liquidation. It was revived by a number of top financiers, including amongst them Alfred Krupp the industrialist. So as not to be confused with the aircraft company LVG, the name Roland was added to the chosen name for the company of LFG creating the company LFG Roland.

The name Roland was chosen because it was said to represent reliability and strength and was named after the medieval commander of the rear-guard of Charlemagne's army, who died a hero's death in the last stand in the Pass of Roncevalles. A statue to Roland is in Bremen.

The first factory opened up at Aldershof, but was destroyed by a mysterious fire on September 6, 1916, said to have been caused by the British Secret Service. The company then moved to Charlottenburg on the outskirts of Berlin, where it continued to manufacture aircraft.

One of the first military aircraft to be produced by LFG Roland, was the C.II, a two-seat reconnaissance model. The C.I had been built by Albatros, so when LFG produced its own aircraft, its designation automatically started with C.II. The fuselage of the C II, because the top wing had been fitted directly to the top of the fuselage, was considered by some to possibly cause problems in control. To precipitate the problem the airframe was fitted to a structure that in turn was mounted on top of a flat-top railway wagon and a series of fast runs made on a long stretch of very fast straight track. It had been hoped that this method would have saved many hours of wind-tunnel testing, but the results obtained were inconclusive.

The design of the fuselage of the C.II was a departure from the traditional method. It was of a semi-monocoque construction and was built on a skeleton

LFG Roland C.II outside the Linke-Hoffman Werk.

of spruce longerons and plywood formers. The fuselage was covered with a thin plywood strips which was spirally wound on to the frame then glued and pinned. This was then covered in fabric and doped. The unbalanced control surfaces were constructed of steel tube and covered in doped fabric, whilst the other control surfaces were made of wood and covered in doped fabric.

The aircraft had a wingspan of 33 ft 10 in., a fuselage length of 25 ft 4 in. and a height of 9 ft 6 in. Powered by a six-cylinder, in-line, water-cooled 160-hp Mercedes D.III engine, the C.II had a top speed of 103 mph., a relatively slow climb rate of 500 feet per minute and a duration of 4-5 hours. It was armed initially with a manually operated Parabellum machine-gun, but later models were armed with a fixed, forward firing, Spandau machine-gun.

The first prototype of the C.II appeared in October 1915, the brainchild of Dipl. Ing. Tantzen, but was lost on the second test flight due to engine failure. A second model was quickly produced, but problems were discovered in its directional stability which was found to be due to the very thin wings that tended to distort after long periods of flight. There was one serious problem in the design, and that was because the upper wing was attached directly on to the top of the fuselage in front of the pilot, and coupled with the `ear' radiators mounted on either side of the fuselage, it restricted his view on landing. The high wing loading caused the aircraft to have a high sink rate and this, combined with the restricted view, was the cause of many crashes during landing. The majority view of the pilots however, was that it was an excellent aircraft, but very difficult to land. *Hauptmann* Hermann Köhl, when with *Kampfstaffel* 22, wrote,

> In the *Walfisch* we had poor visibility and every pilot was in a sweat about the coming landing.

The first Roland C.IIs were supplied to *Kampfgeschwaders* (Battle Wings) attached to the Fifth Army at Verdun. This was a real baptism-under-fire for the aircraft, for at that moment in time Verdun was in the middle of one of the bloodiest and intensive battle of the war. During the battle one of the C.II

LFG Roland C.II. with the pilot and observer standing in front.

'*Walfisch*' was shot down behind the Allied lines, allowing the Allies the opportunity to inspect the aircraft for the first time. What was interesting, was that the observer's gun was a British made Lewis machine-gun.

A number of *Feldflieger Abteilungs* and *Kampfgeschwaders* were supplied with the aircraft including *Jasta* 27 which at the time, was commanded by *Oberleutnant* Hermann Göring. There was one unit whose aircraft consisted entirely of LFG Roland C.IIs and that was Marine *Feldjagdstaffel* 2. This units aircraft were entirely wiped out a few months after receiving the aircraft, by a British bombardment. Their aircraft were replaced with Albatros D.IIIs. The only armament carried was a manually operated Parabellum machine gun mounted in the observers rear cockpit. One of the Fl. Abt. units was *Flieger Abteilung* 4 commanded by *Hauptmann* Eduard *Ritter* von Schleich, holder of the *Orden Pour le Mérite*, who was also known as the `Black Knight'. A number of Allied airmen who came in contact with these two-seat reconnaissance aircraft had tremendous respect for them. Some of the crews however said the aircraft resembled a whale and gave it the nickname of *Walfisch*.

Another problem came to light after the aircraft had been active on the Front for a few weeks. It was discovered that the C.II *Walfisch* was extremely vulnerable from attacks from below. Captain Albert Ball, V.C., was one of the first to exploit this discovery. By diving under the C.II he would come up beneath the aircraft and with his upper wing-mounted Lewis gun in an almost vertical position, attack his adversary. Because of the restricted downward view brought about by the high fuselage, broad `I' struts and upper wing position, visibility beneath the aircraft was partially blocked.

The C.II was involved in a number of escapades including one daring mission behind the Russian lines. *Oberleutnant* Maximillian von Cossel and his pilot *Leutnant* Rudolf Windisch were convinced that the could blow up the rail line that ran to the fortified city of Rowno. This was the only secure method of

LFG Roland 'Walfisch' in 1915.

communication to the city and a number of bombing raids had failed to destroy it. The two airmen decided to fly their aircraft in at night, land in a field nearby, where von Cossel, dressed like a peasant, would get out and plant the explosives along the track. In the meantime Windisch would take off and return to base, but returning the following night to pick up von Cossel at a prearranged time. The explosives were detonated by means of a timer device causing great disruption to the city of Rowno.

In another incident on the night of 6/7 November 1916, *Hauptmann* Hermann Köhl, led his *Bombengeschwader* 7 on a raid and destroyed one of France's largest ammunition dumps at Cerisy.

The exact number of LFG Roland C.IIs that were built and supplied to the army is not known, but it is believed to be several hundred. A number

LFG Roland C.II Specifications

Performance

Wingspan:	33 ft 10 in.
Length:	25 ft 4 in.
Height:	9 ft 6 in.
Weight Empty:	1,680lb
Weight Loaded:	2,824lb.
Maximum Speed:	103 mph.
Ceiling:	14,600 ft.
Duration:	4 - 5 hours.
Armament:	One manually operated Parabellum machine-gun mounted in the observers cockpit and one forward-firing synchronised Spandau machine-gun.
Engine:	One 160-hp Mercedes D.III six-cylinder, in-line, water-cooled.

of these aircraft were built under licence by the Linke-Hoffman company under the designation of Roland C.IIa (Li).

Linke-Hoffman were chosen because of the company's extensive woodworking skills and their already considerable experience with aircraft production.

LFG Roland D.II with the pilot about to start his engine.

An improved model of the C.II was produced early in 1916 powered by a 200-hp Benz Bz. IV engine. Only the one model was built and that was destroyed in the fire when the factory at Aldershof was burnt down. Fortunately the patterns, jigs and dies were all saved, along with a number of fuselages.

Not to be deterred by the fire, the company started producing aircraft again within twenty-four hours after moving to their new factory in the centre of Berlin. The company then decided to produce a single-seat fighter, the LFG Roland D.I The success of the C II had given rise to the development of the new aircraft. Looking like a slimmer, more rakish model of the C.I the D.I was powered by the 160-hp Mercedes D.III engine which gave the aircraft a top speed of 105 mph. The appearance of the D.I, gave rise to its name of *Haifisch* (Shark), which was in direct contrast to the C.II *Walfisch* (Whale) upon which it was based.

The D.I and D.II were powered by the same engine, although another engine was tried later, the 180-hp Argus As.III, which produced the D.IIa. This gave the aircraft a top speed of 105 mph and a climb rate of 800 feet per minute.

Both the D.I and D.II had minor differences in their construction, but in the main they were almost identical. Over three hundred of these aircraft were built, but surprisingly the vast majority of these were built by the *Pfalz Flugzeug-Werke* under licence. With a wingspan of 29 ft 4 in., a fuselage length of 22 ft 9 in., and a height of 10 ft., both aircraft were armed with

LFG Roland D.II.

two fixed, forward firing Spandau machine-guns.

LFG Roland D.II & IIa Specifications

Performance

Wingspan:	29 ft 4 in. (D.II) 29 ft 3 in. (D.IIa)
Length:	22 ft 9 in. (D.II) 22 ft 10 in. (D.IIa)
Height:	10 ft 3 in. (D.II) 9 ft 8 in. (D.IIa)
Weight Empty:	1,573lb. (D.II) 1,397lb. (D.IIa)
Weight Loaded:	2,098lb. (D.II) 1,749lb. (D.IIa)
Maximum Speed:	105 mph.
Ceiling:	14,600ft.
Duration:	4 - 5 hours.
Armament:	Two forward-firing synchronised Spandau machine-guns.
Engine:	D.II; One 160-hp Mercedes DIII 6-cylinder, in-line, water-cooled. D.IIa; One 180-hp Argus As III 6-cylinder, in-line, water-cooled.

In October 1916 the D.III appeared as a replacement for the D.IIa. Unfortunately it appeared at the same time as the superior Albatros fighter and only a small number were ever built. Its specifications were the same as that of the D.IIa.

The C series continued to be built, but with no C.IV model, a prototype two-seater based on the D.II design was produced. The C.V model was powered by a 160-hp Mercedes engine and armed with one fixed, forward firing Spandau machine-gun and one manually operated Parabellum machine-gun mounted in the observers cockpit. Only one aircraft was built.

The first, and the last, of the LFG triplanes was built at the beginning of 1917, the single-seat LFG Roland D.IV. It had a number of unusual features including a tailplane that could be adjusted for incidence prior to flight and it had ailerons fitted to both upper and lower wings. It was powered by a 160-hp Mercedes engine and was one of the most elegant looking of all the triplanes built. It is not known how many were built.

The success of the D.I model prompted the Navy to request a single-seat seaplane. A converted D.I, the LFG WD was produced and powered by a 160-hp Mercedes engine, had its first flight on 29 June 1917. It was not the success hoped for and only the one prototype was built. There had been an earlier seaplane built by LFG, the LFG W, but it was no more than an Albatros C.Ia two-seat reconnaissance model that LFG had built under licence. Only one of

LFG Roland D.IIs of Jasta 25 in Macedonia.

this type was built.

Continuing with the D series, the D.V model, a development of the D.III was produced. The fuselage, although based on the previous models, was a considerably slimmer. It was powered by a 160-hp Mercedes engine. Only one

LFG Roland D.II of Jasta 25 in Macedonia in 1917.

Manfred von Richthofen in the cockpit of an LFG Roland D.IV at Aldershof about to take off on a test flight.

prototype was built.

The last of the original design two-seaters, the C.VIII, was built at the end of 1917. Based on the design of the C.III, it was powered originally by a 260-hp Mercedes D.IVa engine, but then later by 245-hp Maybach Mb.IV engine. It carried one forward firing Spandau machine gun and one manually operated Parabellum machine gun mounted in the rear cockpit.

One of the best fighter aircraft from the LFG stable was the LFG Roland D.VIa. With its distinctive `clinker-built' fuselage and droopy nose, it presented a sleek racy look that was backed up with good performance.

The fuselage was constructed in the same manner as a small boat, with slightly tapered strips of spruce wood overlapping each other by two-thirds. It had a large horn-balanced rudder and overhung balanced ailerons. Powered by a six-cylinder, in-line, water-cooled Benz Bz. IIIa engine, which gave the D.VIa a top speed of 114 mph and a climb rate of about 1,000 feet per minute.

The prototype D.VI, the production models were designated D.VIas, marked the 1,000th LFG Roland aircraft built. The LFG Roland D.VIa had a wingspan of 30ft. 10in., a fuselage length of 20 ft 9 in. and a height of 9 ft 3 in. A number of the aircraft were operational with *Jagdstaffeln* (*Jasta* 23), the remainder saw service with the German Navy being used for seaplane defence duties.

Another prototype model, there were three in all, which was a standard D.VIb, was fitted with two-bay wings with `**I**' interplane struts. Only one was built.

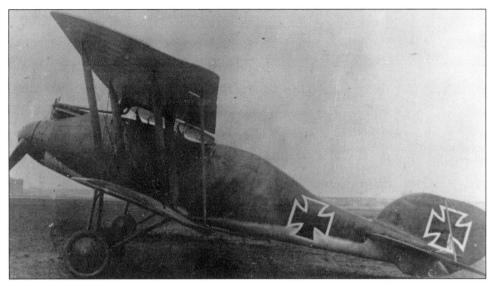

LFG Roland C.VIII.

Two prototypes of the LFG Roland D.VII appeared at the beginning of 1918, the first No. 224/18, was fitted with a 195-hp Benz.IIIb direct-drive engine, which gave it a top speed of 108 mph. The second, No. 3910/18, which had differently shaped and balanced ailerons, was also fitted with a 195-hp Benz.IIIb engine, although this model had reduction gears to decrease the airscrew speed. Only one of each model was built.

Three D.IX prototypes appeared just after the D.VIIs but were different in every respect. The first version, No. 3001/18, was fitted with a 160-hp Siemens-

The first version of the LFG Roland D.VIa in the workshops.

The second version of the LFG Roland D.VIa.

Halske Sh.III geared rotary engine that turned a four-bladed airscrew. It was also fitted with overhung balanced ailerons. This was the first time a rotary engine had been used by the LFG company.

The second of the prototypes had much larger tail surfaces and had a 210-hp Siemens-Halske IIIa geared rotary engine installed. The third version was almost identical to the second, the only difference being the fitting of a large horn-balanced rudder. All three versions were fitted with twin fixed, forward

The LFG Roland D.VIb with its 'clinker' style wooden fuselage.

firing Spandau machine-guns.

The D.X series started with the D.XIII, there appears to have been no D.X, X.I or X.II. This in fact was no more than a re-engined D.VII with a 195-hp V-8 Korting engine with reduction gearing.

The arrival of the LFG Roland D.XIV, No. 300/18, coincided with the installation of a power plant, the 170-hp Goebel Goe IIIa rotary engine. Four new versions of the LFG Roland D.XV., the first two using the D.VI airframe, were produced in May 1918. The first, No. 3004/18, incorporated the D.IV 'clinker-built' fuselage. The wings had a considerable stagger and were braced by twin-struts, but no bracing cables were used. It was powered by a 160-hp Mercedes D.III engine, had a wingspan of 28 ft 5 in. Its overall fuselage length was 20 ft 7 in.

LFG Roland D.VII prototype.

The second D.XV version, No.3006/18, used the D.VI airframe and was powered by a 180-hp Mercedes D.IIIa engine. The wings were braced by single `I' struts and like the first version, without the use of cables. This was also the last of the LFG Roland fighters to use the `clinker-built' fuselage.

The third version of the D.XV had slab-sided fuselage constructed of plywood. The wings were braced with `N' struts made of tubular steel. The engine was a 185-hp BMW III giving the aircraft a top speed of 105 mph. The fourth version, which was almost identical, was fitted with a 200-hp Benz Bz IIIa V engine which gave the aircraft a top speed of 108 mph.

Inspired by the success of the Fokker E.V fighter, LFG Roland produced the D.XVI. This was a parasol fighter with a plywood covered fuselage and fabric covered wings. The D XVI was powered by a 160-hp Siemens-Halske Sh.III rotary engine which drove a four-bladed airscrew. A second version was produced which had slightly differently shaped vertical tail surfaces. The engine was also changed to the 170-hp Goebel Goe.III rotary.

Just before the Armistice - the last in a long line of LFG Roland fighters appeared, the D. XVII. A parasol fighter, it incorporated the same fuselage and power plant as the D XV prototype. It was armed, as all the previous fighters were, with twin, forward-firing, synchronised Spandau machine-guns.

There was one attempt at producing a bomber - the LFG Roland G.I. Although having two propellers, it was in fact a single-engined aircraft turning both the propellers through a complicated system of gears and shafts. The aircraft was also fitted with heavy duty tyres and had twin nose-wheels. It was powered by a 245-hp Maybach Mb.IV engine, had a wingspan of 98 ft 10 in., a fuselage length 52 ft. 2 in., and had a top speed of 100 mph. It carried a crew of two and was armed with one manually operated Parabellum machine gun mounted in the rear cockpit.

The same year, LFG put forward a design for a single-seat scout plane that

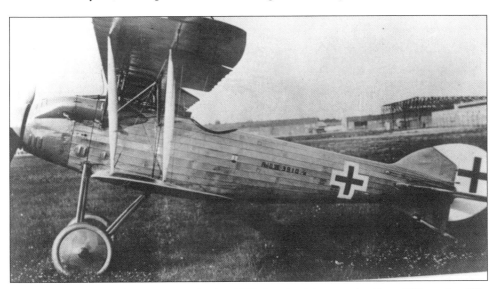

The second version of the LFG Roland D.VII fitted with a 195-hp Benz IIIb engine. The armament was two Spandau machine-guns.

could be carried on board a submarine. The LFG Stralsund V.19, or *Putbus*, as it was called, was a long wing monoplane built of aluminium and powered by a 110-hp Oberursel rotary engine. The V.19 was a very simply designed aircraft, of which the fuselage was just a tube of flat wrapped duraluminium. The wings held all the fuel and had automatic shut-off valves that enabled the wings to be removed without first draining the tanks.

Weighing 1056 lbs empty and with a wingspan of 31ft, the Putbus could reach

LFG Roland D.IX.

a speed of 112mph. Although initially the V.19 Putbus appeared to be better than the Hansa-Brandenburg W-20, which had been an earlier attempt to put an aircraft on a submarine, this was proved not to be so. The main problem, was that it took ten times longer to assemble and disassemble, and required five waterproof containers to house it. The German Navy's submarine arm was told that it was ready for trials, but then shortly afterwards came defeat for Germany and all such trials and experiments were shelved.

The *Luftfahrzeug Gesellschaft* company contributed a great deal to the German war machine and left behind a legacy in the world of aviation.

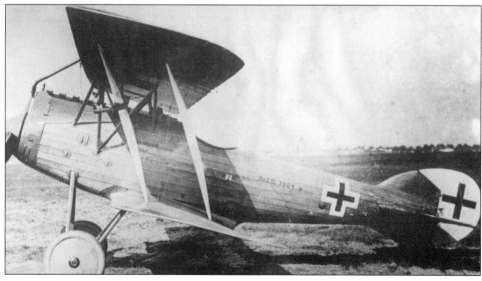

LFG Roland D.XV first version.

LFG Roland D. VIa & D. VIb

Performance

Wingspan:	30 ft 10 in.
Length:	20 ft 9 in.
Height:	9 ft 3 in.
Weight Empty:	1,450lb.
Weight Loaded:	1,892lb.
Maximum Speed:	114 mph.
Ceiling:	19,600 ft.
Duration:	2 hours.
Armament:	Two forward-firing synchronised Spandau machine-guns.
Engine:	One 200-hp Benz Bz IIIa. 6-cylinder, in-line, water-cooled.

LFG Stralsund V.19 'Putbus'. Designed to be carried aboard a submarine but never used.

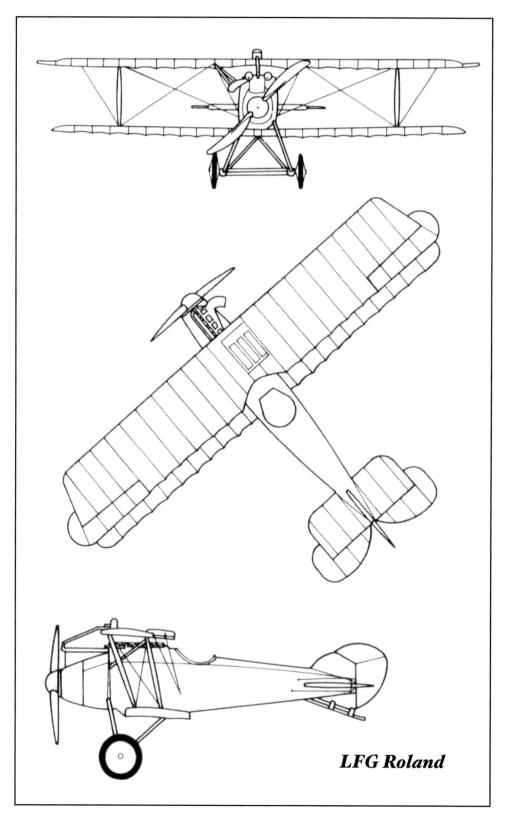

LFG Roland